A PRACTICAL THEOLOGY
OF FAMILY WORSHIP

A PRACTICAL THEOLOGY OF FAMILY WORSHIP

Richard Baxter's Timeless
Encouragement for Today's Home

Jonathan Williams

Reformation Heritage Books
Grand Rapids, Michigan

A Practical Theology of Family Worship
© 2021 by Jonathan Williams

Reformation Heritage Books
3070 29th St. SE
Grand Rapids, MI 49512
616-977-0889
orders@heritagebooks.org
www.heritagebooks.org

Printed in the United States of America
21 22 23 24 25 26/10 9 8 7 6 5 4 3 2 1

Library of Congress Cataloging-in-Publication Data

Names: Williams, Jonathan, (Senior pastor) author.
Title: A practical theology of family worship : Richard Baxter's timeless encouragement for today's home / Jonathan Williams.
Description: Grand Rapids, Michigan : Reformation Heritage Books, [2021] | Includes bibliographical references and index.
Identifiers: LCCN 2021011369 (print) | LCCN 2021011370 (ebook) | ISBN 9781601788856 (paperback) | ISBN 9781601788863 (epub)
Subjects: LCSH: Families—Religious life. | Worship. | Baxter, Richard, 1615-1691.
Classification: LCC BV200 .W55 2021 (print) | LCC BV200 (ebook) | DDC 249—dc23
LC record available at https://lccn.loc.gov/2021011369
LC ebook record available at https://lccn.loc.gov/2021011370

For additional Reformed literature, request a free book list from Reformation Heritage Books at the above regular or email address.

∽⚭

FOR JESS, MY LOVE,
who always fills our home with grace and worship,

FOR GRACIE, SILAS, AND ELIJAH,
who bring me more joy than they will ever know,

AND FOR MY MOM AND DAD,
who first showed me Christ

∽⚭

Contents

Preface

More than 350 years ago, an English pastor set out to encourage family worship and demonstrate that it is God's will for the home. Richard Baxter provided a vision for family worship that is deeply rooted in the Word of God. Not content simply to teach, however, Baxter also equipped families to practice worship together and enjoy the transforming power of Christ in the home, presenting encouragement coupled with practical guidelines for implementing this spiritual discipline.

It was in his book *A Christian Directory* that Baxter presented his most powerful and persuasive argument for family worship. He stood on Scripture and wrote with conviction, believing that such worship honors God and blesses families. This blessing remains for those today who bring the Word of God into their homes.

Baxter's approach was deliberate and orderly, leaning on a systematic outline of propositions, arguments, and Scriptures. As Baxter applied these Scriptures to the discipline of family worship, he also applied them to every Christian home, exhorting households to respond to the biblical call to worship together. This call echoes from generation to generation as an invitation for any Christian who longs to see the transforming power that God's Word can have on families.

Based on the conviction that Baxter's encouragement for family worship continues to speak to the church today, this book is fueled by a desire to examine the biblical portrait of family and God's heart for the home. Each chapter considers how God's Word instructs families concerning their worship together and how they can and

must respond. The prayer is that this book might lead more families
to worship together so that the Lord will be glorified in the home. It
is also offered as an encouragement to those ready to begin practicing and growing in their family worship. It is an exhortation to
lead your family in prayer and praise, to teach the Word of God
in the home, and to enjoy the blessings of worshiping together.
The following chapters celebrate Richard Baxter's bold belief that
family worship is God's will. These chapters are offered with the
prayer that you will allow Baxter's timeless encouragement and
the many Scriptures he stands on to spur you on in a newfound
or perhaps renewed passion for worship in your home.

CHAPTER ONE

The Blessings of Family Worship

Family worship takes place when a Christian household gathers to pray, teach the Word of God, and praise the Lord. Many families today seek to cultivate regular rhythms of worship. In these homes, worship becomes an intentional and joyful response to a biblical call, biblical encouragements, and biblical examples. Blessings await all who seek to bring the gospel into the home.

This spiritual discipline is encouraged and modeled throughout Scripture, yet in our busy, distracted culture it is far too often a lost discipline. After seeing this practice fade in importance over the course of generations, it is time to consider how we can begin to cultivate it in our homes once again. How do we rediscover the joy of family worship?

For many today, the idea of incorporating regular rhythms of worship seems overwhelming. Faithfulness in teaching the Bible in the home, consistency in praying with spouses and children, and regular times of praise may seem out of reach and challenging. However, as families begin these practices, they inevitably become more natural over time, and the challenges are overshadowed by the blessings.

Family worship is rewarding. It brings blessings as you find your family members sharing their hearts with one another. It will afford you opportunities to hear your children talk about Jesus while growing in their love for the Lord. It will allow you space to speak words of confession, forgiveness, and grace to one another. Family worship opens up the door to prayers for daily bread, thanksgiving, and restoration. It is one of the most powerful ways we can usher the gospel of Christ into our homes as we pray that the Lord will open up our hearts to receive it as well. This is one of the greatest opportunities to enjoy the transforming power of Christ in our homes.

A Case for a Practical Theology of Family Worship

Conversations regarding family worship quickly highlight passages such as Deuteronomy 6:4–9, Joshua 24:15, and Ephesians 6:4. While these texts strongly support the church's understanding of family worship, they should not stand alone. A call to teach the Word of God in the home and examples of this discipline are all presented frequently in the Bible. Baxter's encouragement for family worship interacts with more than fifty biblical passages, demonstrating that it is not an insignificant discipline or minor theme of Scripture. Instead, Baxter proves that this form of worship is expected and directed; therefore, it should exist and thrive in Christian homes today.

Instead of treating theology and family worship as separate fields, Baxter viewed the two subjects synoptically, putting them side by side. John Frame proposed, "There really is no justification for restricting theology only to academic or technical questions.... Practical questions are equally grist for the theologian's mill."[1] This certainly seems to fit with Baxter's approach and his understanding of his work in *A Christian Directory*. The original title presented his work as "a sum of practical theology," which may be understood as a comprehensive study that concerns "all that is involved with living before God as a faithful disciple of Jesus Christ."[2]

We will follow Baxter's understanding of a broad definition of theology, one that confronts both the biblical and practical considerations of family worship. Our study will focus on a comprehensive view of relevant Scriptures and their implications for and applications

---

1. John M. Frame, *Systematic Theology: An Introduction to Christian Belief* (Phillipsburg, N.J.: P&R Publishing, 2013), 8.

2. Richard Baxter, *The Godly Home*, ed. Randall J. Pederson (Wheaton, Ill.: Crossway, 2010), 10–11.

of family worship. Therefore, for the purpose of this book, the following definition of theology will be adopted: "Theology is the application of Scripture, by persons, to every area of life."[3] A theology of family worship is developed, therefore, as Baxter applied Scripture to this discipline.

This approach was also considered practical. Rather than considering family worship theoretically or merely confronting ideas about it, Baxter sought to apply the Word of God to actual families in a very practical way. He hoped to spur them on to action. This is the same hope for this book, for the prayer is that families would grow not only in knowledge about household worship but in its practice as well.

Baxter's treatment of this discipline proved to be nothing less than an in-depth biblical study. As he engaged dozens of Scriptures in his encouragement of family worship, he successfully and biblically defended his position that "the solemn worship of God in and by families is of divine appointment."[4] Baxter demonstrated that families enjoy abundant opportunities for family worship, that it brings opportunities for teaching the Word of God, and that it fills the home with prayer and praises.

Throughout church history, family worship used to be commonplace among Christian households as they gathered regularly to read, pray, and sing praises. But nowadays this might seem rare or even foreign, so a few definitions will be helpful in achieving a common understanding of this practice.

Baxter made an important distinction in his definition of *family*. He focused on a household rather than a kindred group or tribe dwelling in many different homes. We will borrow Baxter's definition of an ordained household with one head leading the family.[5]

---

3. Frame, *Systematic Theology*, 8.

4. Baxter, *Godly Home*, 61.

5. Baxter, *Godly Home*, 59. Andreas J. Köstenberger offered a similar yet expanded definition of family that is also appreciated throughout this book. He defined family as "primarily, one man and one woman united in matrimony (barring death of a spouse) plus (normally) natural or adopted children and, secondarily, any other persons related

This simple definition will prove sufficient for examining the theology of the worship taking place within a household and the one leading this time of family worship.

Baxter defined *worship* as "a religious performance of some sacred actions, with an intention of honoring God as God, and that more directly than in common works of obedience."[6] Family worship, therefore, will find families intent on honoring God as God through some sort of sacred action. As with Daniel Block's volume on worship, this book is concerned with Christian worship "committedly monotheistic but also mysteriously Trinitarian, acknowledging the one Triune God as Father, Son, and Holy Spirit."[7]

A Case for Richard Baxter's *Christian Directory*

Richard Baxter (1615–1691) proved to be an avid writer throughout his ministry. J. I. Packer considered Baxter "the most prolific and the most successful of Puritan practical writers."[8] Even in his lifetime, Baxter's works were translated into German and French, being read as far as Switzerland, Germany, France, Hungary, and Poland.[9] Timothy Beougher estimated that Baxter wrote between 141 and 200 books based on various divisions of his writing.[10]

His longest book, consisting of more than one million words, *A Christian Directory*, was published in 1673. He began this intense writing project in 1664 and spent about a year working on it. *A*

---

by blood." Andreas J. Köstenberger with David W. Jones, *God, Marriage, and Family: Rebuilding the Biblical Foundation* (Wheaton, Ill.: Crossway, 2004), 93.

6. Baxter, *Godly Home*, 58.

7. Daniel I. Block, *For the Glory of God: Recovering a Biblical Theology of Worship* (Grand Rapids: Baker Academic, 2014), 2.

8. J. I. Packer, *The Redemption and Restoration of Man in the Thought of Richard Baxter* (Carlisle, U.K.: Paternoster Press, 2003), 55.

9. Packer, *Redemption and Restoration of Man*, 57.

10. Timothy K. Beougher, "Richard Baxter (1615–1691): A Model of Pastoral Leadership for Evangelism and Church Growth," *The Southern Baptist Journal of Theology* 6, no. 4 (Winter 2002), 10. Beougher argued that Baxter wrote 168 books. Geoffrey Nuttall listed 135 books with an additional six posthumous publications. Geoffrey F. Nuttall, *Richard Baxter* (London: Thomas Nelson, 1965), 132–36.

Christian Directory stands out as an encyclopedia of sorts, exploring multiple aspects of the Christian life. The original, lengthy title read, *A Christian Directory or, A Sum of Practical Theology, and Cases of Conscience Directing Christians How to Use Their Knowledge and Faith; How to Improve All Helps and Means, and to Perform All Duties; How to Overcome Temptations, and to Escape or Mortify Every Sin; in Four Parts: I. Christian Ethics (or Private Duties); II. Christian Economics (or Family Duties); III. Christian Ecclesiastics (or Church Duties); IV. Christian Politics (or Duties to Our Rulers and Neighbors).*

The second part of this directory deals with family worship. Baxter's deeply rooted and extensively defended belief that family worship is God's will shaped his entire pastoral ministry and motivated him as he spent his tenure in Kidderminster, England (1641–1642 and 1647–1660), equipping families through preaching, home visits, catechisms, and counseling. In their evaluation of this aspect of the Puritan movement, Joel Beeke and Mark Jones wrote, "So seriously did the Puritans take the duty of family worship that they regarded the neglect of family devotion and catechism to be covenant-breaking with God, and betraying the souls of their children to the devil."[11]

Baxter's ministry to families remains an important case study for several reasons and will receive attention throughout the following chapters. His tenure as pastor in Kidderminster enjoyed a revival of family worship, which Joel Beeke and Randall Pederson put into perspective: "When Baxter came to Kidderminster, scarcely one family on each street among the 800 families honored God in family worship. By the end of his ministry, there were streets on which every family did so."[12] Beeke and Jones also noted, "Christians have long recognized that God often uses the restoration of family worship to bring reformation and revival to the church."[13] Baxter's theology

---

11. Joel R. Beeke and Mark Jones, *A Puritan Theology: Doctrine for Life* (Grand Rapids: Reformation Heritage, 2012), 864.

12. Joel R. Beeke and Randall J. Pederson, *Meet the Puritans: With a Guide to Modern Reprints* (Grand Rapids: Reformation Heritage, 2006), 64.

13. Beeke and Jones, *Puritan Theology*, 864.

of family worship, as presented in his *Christian Directory*, remains useful. As Beeke and Jones suggested, "No Puritan work on applied theology has surpassed this treatise."[14]

Packer asked, "Is it important for later generations to remember Baxter? In 1875 Kidderminster they thought it was, and a fine statue of him preaching was erected in the town center, with the following inscription: Between the years 1641 and 1660 this town was the scene of the labors of Richard Baxter renowned equally for his Christian learning and pastoral fidelity. In a stormy and divided age he advocated unity and comprehension pointing the way to the everlasting rest. Churchmen and nonconformists united to raise the memorial, A.D. 1875."[15]

Packer concluded with this plea: "Get to know Baxter and stay with Baxter. He will always do you good."[16]

---

14. Beeke and Jones, *Puritan Theology*, 938.

15. J. I. Packer, *Puritan Portraits* (Fearn, Ross-shire, U.K.: Christian Focus Publications, 2012), 160–61.

16. Packer, *Puritan Portraits*, 178.

CHAPTER TWO

Historical Examination of Baxter's Context as a Seventeenth-Century English Puritan

Who Were the Puritans?

To truly engage Richard Baxter's theology of family worship, one must recognize the context in which he served and wrote. Baxter is remembered as one of the leading characters of the Puritan movement in seventeenth-century England. We can better understand his passion for the home as we consider the background of the Puritan movement and its impact on his view of family worship.

While Baxter's culture and ours prove widely different, the biblical mission to lead our families in family worship has never changed. It is a call that reaches every generation, for family worship is a timeless discipline. It blessed the families in Baxter's church, and it continues to bless families today.

Although Baxter remains one of the foremost examples of a Puritan who equipped his church in family worship, the Puritan movement began nearly a century before Baxter was born. Leland Ryken traced the history of Puritanism back to 1526 with leaders such as William Tyndale and Hugh Latimer. During this movement, the Puritans valued family worship with the husband/father as the spiritual head of the household. Ryken wrote, "According to the Puritans, the primary purpose of a family is to glorify God."[1] This purpose was fulfilled through bringing the church into their homes, catechizing, and family worship. "Worship was a regular part of the household routine."[2]

---

1. Leland Ryken, *Worldly Saints: The Puritans as They Really Were* (Grand Rapids: Zondervan, 1990), 73.

2. Ryken, *Worldly Saints*, 85.

D. M. Lloyd-Jones also asserted that Puritanism began with Tyndale. While the term *Puritan* may not have appeared until 1567, Puritanism itself began decades earlier. Lloyd-Jones wrote, "The great characteristics of Puritanism began to show themselves in Tyndale."[3] Lloyd-Jones rejected what he referred to as the "Anglican view" of Puritanism, which holds that Puritanism began much later in the 1570s with men such as Richard Greenham and Richard Rogers.[4]

Packer defined Puritanism as a "movement in sixteenth and seventeenth century England which sought further reformation and renewal in the Church of England."[5] Ryken expanded on this definition, remembering the Puritans as those who "wished to purify the church of the remaining vestiges of Catholic ceremony, ritual, and hierarchy."[6]

While the term *Puritan* began as an insult meant to criticize and abuse, it has since become one of affection and respect. Packer noted, however, that "those who identified with this movement did not call themselves Puritans nor welcome the label when others applied it to them."[7] Packer identified Baxter as a mid-period Puritan, although he was quick to note that Baxter would not have applied this term to himself. Those who opposed Baxter did call him a Puritan, as seen by two men attempting to insult him with the term in 1680. They printed their attack in Latin, accusing him of being "a dyed-in-the-wool Puritan and one who oozed the whole of Puritanism from every pore."[8] Baxter, however, preferred to summarize his position as "mere Christianity," a phrase later borrowed by C. S. Lewis.[9]

---

3. D. M. Lloyd-Jones, *The Puritans: Their Origins and Successors* (Carlisle, Pa.: Banner of Truth, 2016), 240.

4. Lloyd-Jones, *Puritans*, 239.

5. J. I. Packer, *A Quest for Godliness: The Puritan Vision of the Christian Life* (Wheaton, Ill.: Crossway, 1990), 35.

6. Ryken, *Worldly Saints*, 7.

7. Packer, *Puritan Portraits*, 12.

8. J. I. Packer, Evangelical *Influences: Profiles of Figures and Movements Rooted in the Reformation* (Peabody, Mass.: Hendrickson, 1999), 24.

9. Packer, *Evangelical Influences*, 158. C. S. Lewis attributes the phrase "mere

John Murray described the Puritans as a brotherhood. The early movements found men familiar with the Reformed churches of Switzerland suddenly confronted with a lack of reformation in England. This remained evident through church practices such as the Prayer Book, indiscriminate ordination, and a lack of preaching. A desire for further reformation began to grow and shape a movement. Murray reported an early list of twenty-eight clergymen who began to separate from some of these practices. This included Thomas Lever, William Whittingham, and Laurence Humphrey. Murray wrote, "Among those clergy we have the makings of a party that was later to be branded Puritan."[10]

Opposition against such Puritans began as early as 1566, when some ministers in London were suspended from ministry for not adhering to legislation requiring specific vestments. By 1570, Thomas Cartwright was expelled from Cambridge University for speaking against the existing offices of the church while advocating for a pattern that followed the biblical model of elders and deacons.[11] Sixteen years later, the Book of Discipline put forth a new model of congregational worship with a biblical view of the sacraments and a central view of preaching. This book was shared among like-minded ministers.[12]

The Book of Discipline followed the model practiced by Reformed and disciplined churches in Geneva. However, Queen Elizabeth (1533–1603) demanded strict observance to the Book of Common Prayer under her Act of Uniformity. In 1593 hundreds of ministers were suspended on accusations of disloyalty to Queen Elizabeth as they refused to use the mandated Book of Common Prayer. Despite this attack, ejected pastors continued to preach in

Christianity" to Baxter in the preface of his book: C. S. Lewis, *Mere Christianity* (New York: Touchstone, 1996), 6.

10. John J. Murray, "The Puritan Brotherhood," in *The Westminster Conference 1991: Advancing in Adversity* (London: Westminster Conference, 1991), 65.

11. Murray, "Puritan Brotherhood," 66.

12. Kelly M. Kapic and Randall C. Gleason, *The Devoted Life: An Invitation to the Puritan Classics* (Downers Grove, Ill.: InterVarsity Press, 2004), 19.

homes and lectureships, while Puritans such as William Perkins continued to preach to groups of Cambridge students.[13]

By 1603, Puritans enjoyed renewed hope for reformation when James I (1566–1625) took the throne. His Calvinism encouraged Puritans to present the Millenary Petition (1603), including the support of more than one thousand clergymen, all petitioning the king for changes to the sacraments and church government. One year later, however, James I demanded conformity to the Church of England. He did pledge to publish a new Bible translation (the King James Version Bible) but left ninety more ministers suspended over the following five years. This suspension included William Ames in 1609 and other leading figures of the early years of the Puritan movement such as Laurence Chaderton, Richard Sibbes, and Richard Greenham.[14] These men championed many of the Puritan values that drove Baxter's ministry more than fifty years later.

In 1643, more than one hundred Puritan ministers met as part of the Westminster Assembly, which gathered frequently between 1643 and 1649. The most notable impact of these sessions came in 1647 when the Westminster Confession of Faith was completed.[15] The thirty-three chapters of the confession addressed Scripture, the sovereignty of God, the fall of man, and salvation in Jesus Christ. A shorter and larger catechism were also included.[16]

While the Puritans shared core doctrines of the faith, they also represented a diversity in their theological convictions. As Mark Deckard noted, the Puritan movement included "Anglicans (William Perkins, Richard Sibbes), Separatists (William Bradford),

---

13. Kapic and Gleason, *Devoted Life*. For a more in-depth treatment of the Puritan movement during the reign of Queen Elizabeth, consider Lloyd-Jones, *Puritans*, 247–54.

14. Kapic and Gleason, *Devoted Life*, 19–20; and Murray, "Puritan Brotherhood," 69.

15. Paul P. Enns, *The Moody Handbook of Theology* (Chicago, Ill.: Moody Press, 1989), 477–78.

16. Jack Rogers, *Presbyterian Creeds: A Guide to the Book of Confessions* (Louisville, Ky.: Westminster John Knox Press, 1991), 155.

Independents (Thomas Goodwin, John Cotton, John Owen), Presbyterians (Thomas Watson) and Baptists (John Bunyan)."[17]

This diversity notwithstanding, a unity remained among the Puritan values. Packer identified four hallmarks shared by the Puritans as he traced their influence back to various Christian leaders. He suggested that Tyndale influenced the Puritans' biblicism, while John Bradford framed their pietism. John Calvin is said to have helped shape the Puritan view of the church, as John Knox did the same for the Puritan view of the world.[18] Through it all, Packer believed Baxter proved to be "the most consistent Puritan" and a "Puritan thoroughbred."[19]

Packer's lengthy description of the Puritans remains helpful as his long list of their values offers the reader a more complete picture of Puritanism: "Puritanism according to Baxter...was a total view of Christianity, Bible-based, church-centered, God-honoring, Christ-exalting, Reformational, internationalist, literate, orthodox, and pastoral.... Puritans saw themselves as God's pilgrims, travelling home through rough country; God's warriors, battling the world, the flesh, and the devil; and God's servants, under orders to worship, fellowship, and do all the good they could as they went along. Of this Christianity Baxter was a masterful teacher and shining example throughout the more than fifty years of his ministerial career."[20]

Ryken's chapter on the family explores this Puritan dynamic of Christian values, specifically interacting with Baxter's views and implementation of family worship. Ryken summarized the Puritans' application of their theology: "Beginning with the premise that the purpose of a family is to glorify God, the Puritans attempted to make their families a 'little church.' The family was ideally a place of sanctified relationships and the mutual worship of God."[21]

---

17. Mark Deckard, *Helpful Truth in Past Places: The Puritan Practice of Biblical Counseling* (Fearn, Ross-shire, U.K.: Mentor, 2016), 12.

18. Packer, *Quest for Godliness*, 329–30.

19. Packer, *Redemption and Restoration of Man*, 99.

20. Packer, *Evangelical Influences*, 226–27.

21. Ryken, *Worldly Saints*, 87.

Beeke and Jones also emphasized the importance of the family in the Puritan movement. The Puritans saw a direct relation between the spiritual health of the family and that of the church: "Usefulness in the church is wedded to godliness in the home."[22] For this reason, the Puritans said, "It is in the home that our spiritual life thrives or fails."[23] Beeke recognized the emphasis on ministry in the home, especially in light of opposition to the Puritan movement. He observed, "The more their public efforts to purify the church were crushed, the more the Puritans turned to the home as a bastion for religious instruction and influence."[24]

Beeke recognized the Puritans' focus on the home as a mainstay for religious instruction. This is evident in their writings on family worship as well as their practice of such.[25] He noted the role of catechizing within the family as well as the Puritan view that the absence of worship in the home served as "evidence of an unconverted life."[26] Beeke defined the Puritan view of "theological foundations of family worship." He wrote,

> The theological foundations of family worship are rooted in the very being of God…. The majestic triune God didn't model Himself after our families; rather, He modeled the earthly concept of family after Himself. Our family life faintly reflects the life of the Holy Trinity. That's why Paul speaks of 'the Father of our Lord Jesus Christ, of whom the family in heaven and earth is named' (Eph. 3:14–15). The love among the persons of the Trinity was so great from eternity that the Father determined to create a world of people who, though finite, would

22. Beeke and Jones, *Puritan Theology*, 859.

23. Beeke and Jones, *Puritan Theology*, 859.

24. Joel R. Beeke, *Puritan Evangelism: A Biblical Approach*, 2nd ed. (Grand Rapids: Reformation Heritage, 2017), 65.

25. Sylvia Brown's 1994 dissertation claimed that treatises written on household government in the seventeenth century were "produced almost exclusively by Puritan divines." Sylvia Monica Brown, "Godly Household Government from Perkins to Milton: The Rhetoric and Politics of Oeconomia, 1600–1645," (PhD diss., Princeton University, 1994), 13.

26. Beeke, *Puritan Evangelism*, 66.

have personalities that reflected the Son. Being conformed to the Son, people could then share in the blessed holiness and joy of the Trinity's family life.[27]

Puritan Views of Family Worship

Puritanism represents a large group of ministers, a variety of doctrinal positions, several locations, and many significant events spanning the course of multiple centuries. However, family worship is one common thread woven throughout this diverse group of leaders and their unique ministries.

Family worship was held in high esteem by the seventeenth-century English Puritans and considered a chief priority. Religious historian Horton Davies explored its role in Puritan life and noted that the head of the family "was in duty bound to teach his children the Scriptures, to lead them and instruct them…and was expected to expound the catechism to his family every Lord's day."[28] J. I. Packer expounded on this further, writing, "Daily and indeed twice daily, the Puritans recommended, the family as a family should hear the word read, and pray to God."[29]

Matthew Henry, like Baxter, was a nonconformist Puritan pastor in the seventeenth century who championed the vision of family worship. Henry echoed Baxter on many levels, speaking on the biblical motivations of family worship as well as the practical method of catechizing one's children. Henry declared, "Let all I have in my house, and all I do in it, be for the glory of God."[30]

The Puritans' view of family worship within the home grew out of their view of general worship within the church. This is evident in the Puritans' view of the regulative principle. W. Young's article "The

---

27. Joel R. Beeke, *Family Worship* (Grand Rapids: Reformation Heritage, 2009), 3.

28. Horton Davies, *The Worship of the English Puritans* (Morgan, Pa.: Soli Deo Gloria Publications, 1997), 278–79.

29. Packer, *Quest for Godliness*, 255.

30. Matthew Henry, *A Church in the House: Restoring Daily Worship to the Christian Household* (San Antonio, Tex.: Vision Forum, 2007), 32. Henry preached this sermon on April 16, 1704.

Puritan Principle of Worship" addresses the "importance of the regulative principle of worship for the origin and essential character of the Puritan movement."[31] Young argued that the Puritan principle of worship "stands out in contrast to the Lutheran view which held that what is not forbidden in the Word of God may be allowed in the worship of God."[32] The Puritans, then, would support introducing only practices and methods of worship that are prescribed by the Word of God. Young attributed the clear expression of the regulative principle to John Calvin, who, in turn, influenced the Puritan view of worship.

The regulative principle proves helpful as one explores Baxter's deep conviction that family worship is in fact prescribed by the Word of God. Young defined this principle by presenting the opposite position: "Opposed to this is subjectivism in worship, where the forms followed arise, not from the revealed will of the Lord, but from the desires, inclinations, imaginations, and decisions of men: and to this the Reformers and Puritans applied the biblical term will-worship."[33]

---

31. W. Young, "The Puritan Principle of Worship," in *Puritan Papers, Volume One: 1956–1959*, ed. J. I. Packer (Phillipsburg, N.J.: P&R Publishing, 2000), 141–53. Daniel I. Block defined the regulative principle as that "which says that true worship involves only components expressly prescribed in Scripture and forbids anything not prescribed" (*For the Glory of God*, 2). Block recognized this sort of teaching in question 51 of the Westminster Shorter Catechism, which interprets the second commandment as teaching that worshiping God by any way not appointed in His Word is forbidden. Likewise, Block noted the 109th question in the Westminster Larger Catechism as teaching the same. He contrasted the regulative principle with the "normative principle, which allows Christians to incorporate in their worship forms and practices not forbidden by Scripture, provided they promote order in worship and do not contradict scriptural principles" (3). Mark Dever continued to write on the regulative principle as he addressed corporate worship in the church. He concluded, "Recognizing the regulative principle amounts to recognizing the sufficiency of Scripture applied to assembled worship." Mark E. Dever, "The Church," in *A Theology for the Church*, ed. Daniel L. Akin (Nashville, Tenn.: B&H Academic, 2007), 811. John Frame defined the regulative principle as that which asserts, "Everything we do in worship must have a biblical basis." Frame, *Systematic Theology*, 1038.

32. Young, "Puritan Principle of Worship," 142.

33. Young, "Puritan Principle of Worship," 147.

Although this view seems to have shaped Baxter's dedication to worship based on Scripture, Packer argued that Baxter proved more flexible than other Puritans. Packer suggested three differing views of worship among the Puritans. These three views consist of a set liturgy, taking advantage of a general manual of direction (perhaps the Westminster Directory[34]), or allowing each minister to regulate the worship of their individual congregations. He claimed that Baxter "approved of a liturgy with room for extempore prayer at the minister's discretion," which he contrasted with John Owen's view that "all liturgies, as such, are false worship."[35]

In an article titled "The Puritan Approach to Worship," Packer wrote on the nature and principles of Puritan worship.[36] He examined the theology of Puritan worship and the foundation of Scripture in their approach, and he also explored the notion that Puritans, like Baxter, biblically defended every aspect of their understanding and practice of worship. The English Puritans shared basic principles about worship: "They agreed that Christian worship must express man's reception of, and response to, evangelical truth, and they were substantially in agreement as to what that truth was. They agreed in analyzing worship as an exercise of mind and heart in praise, thanksgiving, prayer, confession of sin, trust in God's promises, and the hearing of God's Word, read and preached."[37]

The Bible remained the warrant of all practices of worship. Church ceremonies that did not have this biblical foundation were viewed as intrusions and ultimately rejected. The Puritans looked at Jesus's words in John 4:24 and understood worship to be both inward and responsive. "They insisted that worship must be simple and scriptural."[38]

---

34. Some authors considered the Westminster Confession to be "the doctrinal standard for Puritan theology." Kapic and Gleason, *Devoted Life*, 22.

35. Packer, *Quest for Godliness*, 248.

36. J. I. Packer, "The Puritan Approach to Worship," in *Puritan Papers, Volume Three: 1963–1964*, ed. J. I. Packer (Phillipsburg, N.J.: P&R Publishing, 2001), 3–19.

37. Packer, "Puritan Approach to Worship," 5.

38. Packer, "Puritan Approach to Worship," 9.

This simple and scriptural worship consisted of activities in which worship was practiced by the church. These typically included praise, prayer, preaching, the sacraments, church discipline, and catechizing. These activities were practiced in various spheres of worship, including public worship with the church congregation, private worship, and family worship in the home: "Family worship was also, to the Puritans, vitally important. Every home should be a church, with the head of the house as its minister.... Parents must teach their children the Scriptures; all members of the household must be given time and a place to pray."[39]

Worship in the home was also meant to be rooted in the Scriptures. As the Puritans sought to worship together with their families, they found themselves dependent on God's Word. William Perkins, "the patriarch of Puritanism," wrote, "The only rule of ordering the family, is the written Word of God."[40]

While such convictions remained strong throughout the movement, many of the goals of the Puritans were not achieved. Packer wrote, "The Puritans lost, more or less, every public battle that they fought."[41] The Church of England did not undergo the reformation for which the Puritans hoped. Many of the Puritan pastors and leaders were persecuted and even imprisoned. However, in Packer's view, these defeats do not diminish their contributions: "The moral and spiritual victories that the Puritans won by keeping sweet, peaceful, patient, obedient, and hopeful under sustained and seemingly intolerable pressures and frustrations give them a place of high honor in the believers' hall of fame."[42] Some of these spiritual victories, filled with revival both in the church and the home, shine brightly in the life and ministry of Richard Baxter.

39. Packer, "Puritan Approach to Worship," 17.
40. As quoted in Beeke and Jones, Puritan Theology, 860.
41. Packer, Quest for Godliness, 23.
42. Packer, Quest for Godliness, 23.

A Brief Biography of Richard Baxter

Baxter was born in England on November 12, 1615, in the village of Rowton. He was born on the Lord's Day during the hour of morning worship. The Word of God had transformed his father, who then became Baxter's first spiritual mentor.[43] Baxter wrote about his father, "When I was very young his serious speeches of God and the life to come possessed me with a fear of sinning."[44]

Baxter's father introduced Richard to the Scriptures, encouraging him to read the historical books of the Bible. While he did not initially understand the doctrine he was reading, it did acquaint him with a love for God's Word from an early age.[45]

The Lord opened Baxter's eyes when he was fifteen years old. He wrote that at this time, God touched his heart "with a livelier feeling of things spiritual than ever before…and it pleased God to awaken my soul."[46] Doubt of his salvation crept in at times throughout his life and ministry. These doubts led to examination and prayer, which led to assurance. Baxter wrote, "Nothing is so firmly believed as that which hath been sometime doubted of."[47]

Instead of leaving home for university studies, Baxter accepted an offer from Richard Wickstead to live with him in Ludlow and benefit from one-on-one tutelage. Baxter wrote of his relationship with Wickstead, "He was the greatest help to my seriousness in religion that ever I had before, and was a daily watchman over my soul. We walked together, we read together, and we prayed together."[48] However, after just two years in this mentorship, Wickstead gave in to drunkenness and never seemed to recover.[49]

---

43. Richard Baxter, *The Autobiography of Richard Baxter* (New York: E. P. Dutton & Co., 1931), 3–4.
44. Baxter, *Autobiography of Richard Baxter*, 4–5.
45. Baxter, *Autobiography of Richard Baxter*, 5.
46. Baxter, *Autobiography of Richard Baxter*, 6–7.
47. Baxter, *Autobiography of Richard Baxter*, 26–27.
48. Baxter, *Autobiography of Richard Baxter*, 7–8.
49. Baxter, *Autobiography of Richard Baxter*, 8.

Wickstead pushed Baxter toward a profession in the courts, persuading him to move to London. Baxter went but stayed for only one month. His mother was sick and requested him to return. In addition to this request, Baxter resolved to leave London because of the weak preaching in the city. He wrote, "When I saw a stage-play instead of a sermon on the Lord's days in the afternoon, and heard little preaching but what was as to one part against the Puritans, I was glad to be gone."[50]

Baxter returned to his mother, who died later that year on May 10. His father remarried one year later to a Christian woman who lived to be ninety-six years old. Baxter was exposed to nonconformists when he was twenty years old.[51] He respected Christian men in Shrewsbury, admiring their prayers and holy lives, yet these godly men were persecuted by the bishops of the church for their views of nonconformity. Baxter wrote, "I found much prejudice arise in my heart against those that persecuted them, and thought those that silenced and troubled such men could not be the genuine followers of the Lord of love."[52]

Baxter followed this experience with intense studies of his own. He aimed to examine all matters concerning conformity before arriving at his own position. He considered the issues of the Book of Common Prayer, wedding rings, making the cross symbol during baptism, the liturgy, church discipline, the administration of the Lord's Supper,

---

50. Baxter, *Autobiography of Richard Baxter*, 12.

51. According to Packer, there were an estimated 120,000 nonconformists in England during the Puritan movement of the seventeenth century. Packer, *Evangelical Influences*, 27. The terms *nonconformist* and *nonconformity* will appear throughout this book and, according to Joel Beeke and Randall Pederson, can be defined as an "act of refusing to conform to the standard decreed for the national church for faith, worship, or polity.... Nonconformists in England often found themselves at odds with people who professed to hold the same articles of faith. Nonconformity later became a collective term for the various 'free' churches, Presbyterian, Congregational, Methodist, Baptist, etc., in England and Wales, existing outside the established church." Beeke and Pederson, *Meet the Puritans*, 850–51.

52. Baxter, *Autobiography of Richard Baxter*, 15–16.

and much more. During this season of study, Baxter often debated the nonconformists, disputing their inclinations toward separation.[53]

John Thornborough, the elderly bishop of Worcester, ordained Baxter as deacon on December 23, 1638, when he was twenty-three years old. Sidney Rooy, reflecting on the significance of this ordination, wrote that this "began a fifty-three-year ministry that spanned the reigns of Charles I, Oliver Cromwell and his son Richard, Charles II, James II, and reached into that of William III."[54]

Following his ordination, Baxter invested nine months serving as the master of the school in Dudley. He left that position in 1639 when he began to serve as assistant minister to William Madstard at Bridgenorth, Shropshire. It was during this time that Baxter developed an appreciation for nonconformity.[55]

This ministry afforded Baxter an outlet for preaching and the freedom to lead the worship service according to his personal convictions without having to declare a strictly conformist position. Baxter described this balance: "I had a very full congregation to preach to, and a freedom from all those things which I scrupled or thought unlawful. I often read the Common Prayer before I preached, but I never administered the Lord's Supper, nor ever baptized any child with the sign of the cross, nor ever wore the surplice, nor was ever put to appear at any bishop's court."[56] Baxter continued to preach the gospel at Bridgenorth for nearly two years.

Baxter's Ministry Context in Kidderminster (1641–1642 and 1647–1660)

St. Mary's Church in Kidderminster, England, called Baxter to be their pastor in 1641. The church had recently fired their minister for

---

53. Baxter, *Autobiography of Richard Baxter*, 16–17.

54. Sidney H. Rooy, *The Theology of Missions in the Puritan Tradition: A Study of Representative Puritans: Richard Sibbes, Richard Baxter, John Eliot, Cotton Mather & Jonathan Edwards* (Grand Rapids: Eerdmans, 2006), 66.

55. Beeke and Pederson, *Meet the Puritans*, 62.

56. Baxter, *Autobiography of Richard Baxter*, 18.

drunkenness and an ignorance of the Scriptures. Baxter accepted the offer and moved to Kidderminster.[57]

Baxter described the congregation as it was when he began his ministry: "It was a full congregation; an ignorant, rude and reveling people for the greater part, who had need of preaching, and yet had among them a small company of converts, who were humble, godly, and of good conversations, and not much hated by the rest, and therefore the fitter to assist their teacher; but above all, they had hardly ever had any lively, serious preaching among them."[58]

He left Kidderminster after the English Civil War broke out in 1642 and spent time preaching to the soldiers and the people of Coventry. These two years of peaceful ministry were interrupted when Colonel Whalley invited Baxter to serve his regiment as chaplain and the governor gave his consent.[59] The next two years of Baxter's ministry were marked by preaching and correction to those who accepted him and by patient endurance with those who did not.[60] Once Baxter separated from the army, he returned to Kidderminster.[61]

Baxter returned to Kidderminster after receiving an invitation signed by 265 congregants.[62] His second term in Kidderminster enjoyed years of intentional family ministry and revival in nearly every home in town. These years afforded Baxter the freedom to preach and to visit families in their homes, catechize them, and counsel them.

Richard Baxter was thin, lean, and physically weak, enduring debility of the nerves throughout his life.[63] As Baxter began to pas-

---

57. Baxter, *Autobiography of Richard Baxter*, 21–24.

58. Baxter, *Autobiography of Richard Baxter*, 25.

59. Baxter, *Autobiography of Richard Baxter*, 50–52.

60. Baxter specifically mentioned two men who ignored him during this time: Oliver Cromwell and James Berry, a captain who had once been Baxter's friend.

61. Baxter, *Autobiography of Richard Baxter*, 59.

62. Nuttall, *Richard Baxter*, 40.

63. Baxter, *Autobiography of Richard Baxter*, 11. J. I. Packer offered further detail regarding Baxter's physical ailments, which included "a tubercular cough; frequent nosebleeds and bleeding from his finger-ends; migraine headaches; inflamed eyes; all kinds of digestive disorders; kidney stones and gallstones" (*Evangelical Influences*, 30).

tor once again, his physical sicknesses and weaknesses persisted. He wrote of several illnesses that he expected to end in his death, and the physical pain seemed inescapable. Baxter wrote, "In my labors at Kidderminster after my return I did all under languishing weakness, being seldom an hour free from pain."[64] His continued sickness and lifelong weaknesses left him with a continual expectation of death. This proved to be a blessing, however, as it stirred him to preach "as a dying man to dying men."[65]

The pain and opposition notwithstanding, Baxter spent these thirteen years convinced that family worship is God's will. He wrote to pastors, "If you desire the reformation and welfare of your people, do all you can to promote family religion.... You are not likely to see any general reformation, till you procure family reformation."[66]

John Brown provides several unique observations about Baxter's ministry context in Kidderminster. Brown offers the reader his own take on the town where Baxter served for so many years: "If I were asked what, in the year 1646, was one of the most unpromising towns in England to which a young man could be sent, who was starting his career as preacher and pastor, I should feel inclined to point at once to the town of Kidderminster in Worcestershire."[67] Brown described Baxter in a similar manner: "If I were asked, who of all men—taking merely physical reasons into account—would seem to be the most unlikely man to be sent as pastor to this most unlikely and unprom- ising place, I should have said that man was Richard Baxter."[68] In light of Brown's initial remarks, his conclusion speaks volumes: "If I were asked to single out one English town of the 17th century which more almost than any other came under the influence of the Spirit of God; and one preacher who, more than most, was successful in

---

64. Nuttall, *Richard Baxter*, 76.

65. Baxter, *Autobiography of Richard Baxter*, 26.

66. Richard Baxter, *The Reformed Pastor* (Carlisle, Pa.: Banner of Truth, 2005), 100–102.

67. John Brown, *Puritan Preaching in England: A Study of Past and Present* (New York: Charles Scribner's Sons, 1900), 165.

68. Brown, *Puritan Preaching in England*, 167–68.

winning men for Christ, and in organizing a vigorous church life under his pastorate, I should say that town was Kidderminster and that preacher was Richard Baxter."[69]

Baxter's ministry in Kidderminster provided him the context in which he could develop and implement his practical theology of family worship. C. Jeffrey Robinson noted that this view of family worship was shared by other Puritans as well: "Puritans and their heirs developed some of the most mature expressions of the theology and practice of what came to be known as 'family worship.'"[70] Robinson's summary of worship in a Puritan's home on the Lord's Day affirms many of Baxter's premises. This family worship included prayers, psalms of praise, Scripture reading, and catechesis.

Baxter left Kidderminster in 1660. He often preached in London in the following years and was ejected from the Church of England in 1662 by the Act of Uniformity.[71] It was in this same year that Baxter encountered his greatest opposition and persecution. He was arrested on several occasions and spent some time in jail. His belongings were confiscated, including his own bed on which he lay sick. Baxter also faced a charge of sedition. The charge, trial, and verdict proved spurious as the accusation focused on some of Baxter's teachings in his New Testament paraphrase. All that he wrote about the Pharisees and Jewish authorities was twisted and considered a veiled denunciation of England's rulers. The judge presiding over the trial called Baxter

---

69. Brown, *Puritan Preaching in England*, 168–69.

70. C. Jeffrey Robinson Sr., "The Home Is an Earthly Kingdom," in *Trained in the Fear of God: Family Ministry in Theological, Historical, and Practical Perspective*, ed. Randy Stinson and Timothy Paul Jones (Grand Rapids: Kregel, 2011), 119.

71. Beeke and Pederson, *Meet the Puritans*, 64. The 1662 Act of Uniformity "made the Book of Common Prayer mandatory in all public services. Refusal could result in monetary fines or imprisonment." About two thousand Puritan pastors refused, including Baxter, and became certified nonconformists, enduring the consequences. Beeke and Jones, *Puritan Theology*, 776, 3. These two thousand pastors, including Baxter and John Bunyan, made up an estimated one-fifth of English clergy. This season of persecution was lifted under the Toleration Act of 1689. The Act of Uniformity was part of the Clarendon Code, "named after Lord Chancellor Edward Hyde, earl of Clarendon." Kapic and Gleason, *Devoted Life*, 22–23.

"a conceited, stubborn, fanatical dog," deserving to be hanged. The jury reached a guilty verdict immediately, leading to Baxter's eighteen months in jail.[72] He was seventy years old at the time.

In his latter days, Baxter spent his time writing and occasionally preaching near Charterhouse Square.[73] Even in his final year of life, he opened the doors of his house twice a day and welcomed any who desired to join him for family worship. His last days found him confined to his room and eventually to his bed. On the day before he died, Baxter spoke with two of his friends. He told them, "I have pain, there is no arguing against sense, but I have peace, I have peace."[74] Baxter's physical infirmities finally overtook him on a Tuesday morning, December 8, 1691. He was seventy-six years old when he died, leaving behind his final words: "O I thank Him, I thank Him; the Lord teach you to die."[75]

---

72. Packer, *Evangelical Influences*, 30.
73. Beeke and Pederson, *Meet the Puritans*, 65.
74. Nuttall, *Richard Baxter*, 112.
75. Marcus L. Loane, *Makers of Puritan History* (Grand Rapids: Baker, 1980), 233.

CHAPTER THREE

Baxter's Encouragement for Family Worship

Baxter saw a call for family worship woven throughout Scripture. He did not believe it was a topic dealt with infrequently, with only a few supporting verses sprinkled throughout the Bible. Instead, Baxter understood that the Word of God provides a robust defense of family worship, championing this discipline time and time again. He was driven by his conviction that the Bible not only commanded it but also offered numerous examples of families practicing such in their homes.

The blessings of family worship are clearly and frequently presented in the Scriptures. Baxter's practical theology of family worship was therefore well-founded on a host of Scriptures, and he presented these systematically as an apologetic for worship in the home. Baxter unfolded his encouragement for this discipline in the form of several propositions consisting of more than thirty arguments. Each argument served to emphasize God's heart for the home as presented in the Bible.

The primary source for Baxter's encouragement for family worship is his book *A Christian Directory*.[1] The second part of this directory deals with family duties, including worship. Baxter applies more than fifty Bible verses in support of his belief that family worship is God's will. At the heart of Baxter's encouragement for family

---

1. Richard Baxter, *A Christian Directory or, A Sum of Practical Theology, and Cases of Conscience, Part 2: Christian Economics* (Independently published, 2018). For the sake of this book, Randall Pederson's edited version will be used, and cited as Baxter, *Godly Home*.

worship is his belief that family worship is God's will for the home and that families are blessed with many occasions for worshiping together.

Families Enjoy Abundant Opportunities for Worship

At the heart of Baxter's encouragement for family worship is his belief that it is God's will for the home and that families are blessed with many occasions for worshiping together. He claimed that "the solemn worship of God in and by families as such is of divine appointment."[2]

Before Baxter unpacked these opportunities, however, he made room for a few disclaimers. First, he noted that family worship will not include every element of worship that takes place in the larger assemblies consisting of an entire church body. Ordinances such as the Lord's Supper and baptism are excluded. Baxter viewed these as fitting only for worship with the church and that they ought to be reserved for such services: "Though some conjecture…that as there is family prayer and church prayer, family teaching and church teaching, so there should be family sacraments and church sacraments, this is a mistake."[3] Baxter draws this conclusion from the lack of any biblical examples of family worship that included these ordinances.

Baxter moved on from these disclaimers in order to present the following five encouragements. Each position biblically defends a theology of family worship, demonstrating that families enjoy abundant opportunities to worship God together.

Family Worship Is Found, Appointed, Used, and Commanded in Scripture

Baxter began his encouragement for family worship as he asserted that it is "found, appointed, used, and commanded in the Scripture."[4] Baxter recognized three aspects of worship that should exist within the home: teaching the Scripture, which includes reading and memorizing (or catechizing) it; teaching the meaning of the Scripture, or

---

2. Baxter, *Godly Home*, 61.
3. Baxter, *Godly Home*, 60.
4. Baxter, *Godly Home*, 70.

explaining it; and applying all that has been taught through reproofs, admonitions, and exhortations.[5]

While the biblical inclusion of family worship serves as the foundation of Baxter's position, other authors, such as Daniel Block, have challenged such a viewpoint. In Block's tome on the theology of worship, he made the provocative claim that biblical support for a pattern of family worship is "embarrassingly limited."[6] This viewpoint stands in stark contrast to Baxter's position that this discipline is found, appointed, used, and commanded throughout Scripture. Block proposed a different view of family worship: "Family worship is best viewed holistically, which means that all domestic activities should involve acts of submission and homage before the divine Sovereign in response to his gracious revelation of himself and in accord with his will.... God is most pleased with the worship of the household and its members when they fulfill the roles God intends for them within the home."[7]

Block maintained that there are few and limited examples of formal family worship in Scripture. He did, however, present biblical examples of this sort of worship, some of which overlap with passages that Baxter presented in his defense. Block recognized the family worship of Noah in Genesis 8:20–9:17, of Job in Job 1:1–5, and of Jacob in Genesis 35:1–15; the domestic flavor of worship during the Passover (Ex. 12–13; 23:14–17; Deut. 16:1–17; Matt. 26:17–25); hints of family worship throughout the book of Deuteronomy (Deut. 6:4–9; 11:18–20; 26:1–15); the worship of Cornelius and a household of believers in Acts 10 and of Lydia's and the Philippian jailer's households in Acts 16; and the discipleship Timothy received through his mother and grandmother (2 Tim 1:5; 3:14–15). Block also mentioned negative illustrations of the lack of family worship in the books of Joshua, Judges, and 1 Samuel. These include Achan's disobedience and the Judges 17 account of Micah, his idolatry, and

---

5. Baxter, *Godly Home*, 71.
6. Block, *For the Glory of God*, 109.
7. Block, *For the Glory of God*, 110.

his self-appointed priest for his family. Block observed, "These were dark days; the Israelites as a nation and as individual households were doing what was right in their own eyes."[8]

Baxter noted several of these same passages in order to demonstrate that family worship is indeed well supported throughout Scripture. The rest of his encouragements explored the patterns and elements of family worship as presented in the Bible. As Scott Brown wrote, "You won't find the words 'family worship' in the Bible, but you can trace its principles and practices from Genesis to Revelation."[9]

Timothy Paul Jones supports Baxter's view that Scripture clearly calls parents to teach Scripture in their homes to their families. Far from agreeing with Block's statements, Jones called this duty a responsibility of Christian parents. He pointed to several Scriptures that command this sort of family teaching. First, Jones noted Deuteronomy 6:6–7, which issues a command that was observed throughout Israel's history. This is seen in other passages such as Joshua 4:6 and Psalm 78:1–7. Jones also recognized the New Testament passage of Ephesians 6:4 as a clear call for "fathers to nurture their children in the training and instruction of the Lord."[10]

Deuteronomy 6 leads many scholars to conclude that family worship is commanded in Scripture. Kerry Ptacek cited this passage as a clear indication that fathers are to teach their children the Word of God in their homes: "God's command that the heads of families teach their children was not vague: God spoke of where, when, and how they were to teach."[11]

Beeke and Jones join Baxter in answering the objection that Scripture does not explicitly call for family worship: "Though there

---

8. Block, *For the Glory of God*, 117.

9. Scott T. Brown and Jeff Pollard, eds., *A Theology of the Family: Five Centuries of Biblical Wisdom for Family Life* (Wake Forest, N.C.: NCFIC, 2016), 45.

10. Timothy Paul Jones, "How a Biblical Worldview Shapes the Way We Teach Our Children," *The Journal of Discipleship and Family Ministry: Equipping the Generations for Gospel-Centered Living* 4, no. 1 (Fall/Winter 2013): 3.

11. Kerry Ptacek, *Family Worship: Biblical Basis, Historical Reality, and Current Need* (Taylors, S.C.: Southern Presbyterian Press, 2000), 9.

is no explicit command, the texts…make clear that God would have families worship him daily."[12] This also seems to reflect the viewpoint of another Puritan, George Hamond (1620–1705), who confronted those who view family worship as an option rather than a duty. While some might consider this a matter of liberty, Hamond considered family worship a discipline required by Scripture. He wrote, "Men are not at liberty whether they will worship God in their families or not."[13]

Families Have Advantages and Opportunities to Worship God

After claiming biblical support for family worship, Baxter continues his encouragement with passages from Matthew, Luke, 1 Corinthians, and 1 Peter. Baxter unfolds his position that family worship is of divine appointment: "If families are societies of God's institution, furnished with special advantages and opportunities for God's solemn worship, having no prohibition not to use them, then the solemn worship of God in and by families as such is of divine appointment."[14] The first part of this argument is assumed. Baxter claimed that no proof is needed to show that "families are societies of God's institution."

He immediately moved on to his claim that families are "furnished with special advantages and opportunities." Families continue to enjoy these abundant opportunities today. Baxter listed seven of these advantages:

1. There is the advantage of authority in the ruler of the family, whereby he may command all who are under him in God's worship.

2. He has the advantage of a singular interest in wife and children, by which he may bring them to it willingly, so that they may perform a right evangelical worship.

---

12. Beeke and Jones, *Puritan Theology*, 872.

13. George Hamond, *The Case for Family Worship* (Orlando, Fla.: Soli Deo Gloria Publications, 2005), 17.

14. Baxter, *Godly Home*, 61.

3. He has the advantage of a singular dependence of all upon him for daily provisions and of his children for their portions for livelihood in the world, whereby he may yet further prevail with them for obedience, he having a power to reward, as well as to punish and command.

4. They have the opportunity of cohabitation and so are still at hand and more together and so in readiness for such employments.

5. Being nearest in relation, they are strongly obliged to further each other's salvation and help each other in serving God.

6. Their nearness of relation and natural affections do singularly advantage them for a more affectionate bond and so for a more forcible and acceptable worship of God when they are in it as of one heart and soul.

7. If any misunderstanding or other impediment arise, they, being still at hand, have opportunity to remove them and to satisfy each other; and if any distempers of understanding, heart, or life be in the family, the ruler, by familiarity and daily converse, is enabled more particularly to fit his reproofs and exhortations, confessions and petitions accordingly, which even ministers in the congregations cannot so well do.[15]

For Baxter, these seven points should convince the reader of the opportunities families have for household worship. He considered his argument well presented: "I have made it evident in this enumeration that families have advantages, yea, special and most excellent advantages and opportunities, for the solemn worship of God."[16]

The final part of the argument states that there are no prohibitions that would keep families from using their advantages and opportunities to worship God together. Baxter simply states that God has not prohibited family worship in the law of nature or the written law, and he challenges any who disagree to prove the opposite. It is,

---

15. Baxter, *Godly Home*, 61–62.
16. Baxter, *Godly Home*, 62.

of course, a rhetorical challenge as Baxter assumes that no one can point to an example of God prohibiting family worship either in the law of nature or the written law.

Therefore, his argument is said to be proven. Baxter wrote, "Families having such advantages and opportunities for God's solemn worship are bound to improve them faithfully for God in the solemn worshipping of him."[17]

Baxter referenced the parable of the talents (Matt. 25:14–30) to defend his position. The application is that talents, advantages, or opportunities are to be faithfully improved on for God. Therefore, families with opportunities to worship together are to improve on this through practice. Luke 20:10 is presented as a reminder that the Lord requires fruit from His vineyard, while Matthew 10:42 is used to show the reader that if the Lord entrusts one with a gift, whether it be a cup of water or opportunity to worship as a family, then He will expect one to give this gift when needed. Likewise, Luke 12:48 is briefly referenced as a call for families to practice faithful stewardship, and 1 Corinthians 4:2 is also quoted for the reader: "Moreover it is required in stewards, that a man be found faithful."[18]

These Scriptures did not receive much commentary. Baxter referenced each one briefly as he applied them to his first argument. He concluded with 1 Peter 4:10–11: "As every man hath received the gift, even so minister the same one to another, as good stewards of the manifold grace of God. If any man speak, let him speak as the oracles of God." Baxter clearly saw the opportunity for family worship as a gift of grace that is to be stewarded; used to produce fruit, given back to the Lord; and used to serve one another.

Family Worship Is of Divine Institution

Baxter continued to encourage families to enjoy their abundant opportunities for household worship. With his third point, he appealed to natural reason. Baxter believed that natural reason shows

---

17. Baxter, *Godly Home*, 62.
18. Baxter, *Godly Home*, 63.

that since God is the founder and instituter of families, they are then to be devoted to Him. This devotion is expressed through family worship. According to Baxter, families "should be for him as well as they are from him,"[19] referencing Romans 11:36: "For of him, and through him, and to him, are all things."

As all things, including families, are made by God and for Him, then their ultimate end must be for God. Baxter referred to this as God's "right of ownership."[20] This right of ownership implies that if God "has a full right of government of families as families, they must honor and worship him according to their utmost capacities."[21] As Jody Anderson noted, "God established the home, and every good Puritan husband was to acknowledge this reality by leading the family in worship."[22]

Thomas Doolittle (1632–1707) was born in Kidderminster and grew up hearing Baxter's preaching. In fact, he was saved through Baxter's sermons that were later published as *The Saints' Everlasting Rest.* Baxter's encouragement led to Doolittle entering the ministry, and he later served as a Puritan preacher as well. Doolittle echoed Baxter's views of God's right of ownership and the implications on family worship. He wrote that God is the founder of all families, and therefore it is the family's duty to worship Him.[23] Beeke and Jones summarized this Puritan position well: "God's right to the worship of our households arises from his sovereignty over each family."[24]

The ownership and headship of God over families rests as the foundation of this argument for family worship. God is the Lord and ruler of families, He is sovereign over them and is therefore deserving

---

19. Baxter, *Godly Home*, 64.

20. Baxter, *Godly Home*, 64.

21. Baxter, *Godly Home*, 64.

22. Jody Kent Anderson, "The Church within the Church: An Examination of Family Worship in Puritan Thought," (PhD diss., Mid-America Baptist Theological Seminary, 2009), 133.

23. Thomas Doolittle, "How May the Duty of Daily Family Prayer Be Best Managed for the Spiritual Benefit of Everyone in the Family?," in *Puritan Sermons, 1659–1689* (Wheaton, Ill.: Richard Owen Roberts, 1981), 2:212.

24. Beeke and Jones, *Puritan Theology*, 865.

of their worship. Baxter concluded with another call to family worship: "If then there is no family whereof God is not the Father or Founder and the Master or Owner and Governor, then there is none but should honor and fear him or worship him, and that not only as single men but as families, because he is not only the Father and Master, the Lord and Ruler of them as men but also as families."[25]

Families Live in the Presence of God and Should Apprehend That Presence

Baxter's next encouragement for family worship repeats the view that "it is God's will that families as such should solemnly worship him." He then states his proposition clearly: "If besides all the opportunities and obligations mentioned before, families do live in the presence of God, they should, by faith, apprehend that presence."[26]

Although God is invisible and unseen in the home, families of faith believe they are walking in His presence daily and that He is present in their homes. Baxter wrote, "Faith sees him who is invisible."[27] So Baxter's argument stands on the foundational principles that God is present with every family and that it is faith which recognizes this presence.

As faith *recognizes* the presence of God within the home, family worship *responds* to this presence. It acknowledges God's presence in an appropriate showing of honor to the true Master of the home. Baxter does not present any supporting Scripture, merely ending this argument with an illustration: "If one of you had a son who was blind and could not see his own father, would you think him excusable if he did not honor his father when he knew him to be present?"[28]

---

25. Baxter, *Godly Home*, 65.
26. Baxter, *Godly Home*, 66.
27. Baxter, *Godly Home*, 66.
28. Baxter, *Godly Home*, 66.

Families Are Societies Sanctified to God

George Hamond also viewed Christian families as societies of God meant for worship. He wrote, "Religious families, being of divine institution, let us observe how that by their very constitution we may perceive an engagement to be laid upon them to worship God together."[29]

Baxter's following argument revisits the idea of families as societies of God, but it shifts the focus from advantages and opportunities to the sanctification of these families. According to Baxter's definition, "To sanctify a person or thing is to set it apart, to separate it from common or unclean use, and to devote it to God, to be employed in his service."[30] Since families are societies of God, they should therefore be set apart for God and devoted to His worship.

This responsibility to worship is referred to as God's third right. Baxter suggested that God has a double right for worship from all humanity since He created them and Jesus died for them, but to the sanctified there is a third right to worship. Families are to devote worship to God, with the alternative presented as nothing less than withholding from God what is due Him. Baxter and other Puritans asked, "What reason or right do we have…to exclude our homes and family times from this call to worship."[31]

Baxter went to the Scriptures for both positive and negative models of those who either failed or were faithful in their worship of God. Ananias was presented as a tragic example of one who withheld from God what should have been devoted to Him (Acts 5:3). Joshua, on the other hand, was offered as a positive example of one who devoted his whole house to God (Josh. 24:15). Abraham also, by circumcision, "consecrated his whole household to God."[32]

The position that Christian families are indeed to be sanctified to God received further support. First, Baxter noted that if Christian

---

29. Hamond, *Case for Family Worship*, 97.
30. Baxter, *Godly Home*, 67.
31. Beeke and Jones, *Puritan Theology*, 865.
32. Baxter, *Godly Home*, 67.

families consist of holy persons, then they are a sanctified society. Second, Scripture presents examples of entire families being devoted to God. This sort of set apart devotion is not reserved for individuals. This is seen in the Passover celebration as families came together as a whole for worship, highlighting their position as sanctified to God. Deuteronomy 7:6 may also serve as another example: "For thou art an holy people unto the LORD thy God: the LORD thy God hath chosen thee to be a special people unto himself, above all people that are upon the face of the earth."

In a similar fashion, New Testament passages apply some of this language to the church, which is God's chosen people, set apart for Him. Baxter noted 1 Peter 2:5–7, 9, which presents Christians as a spiritual house, a royal and holy priesthood, and a chosen generation for God's own possession. This passage demonstrates that God's people are set apart for the purpose of worshiping Him, of proclaiming His excellencies. Baxter summarizes this as "a special dedication of families to God."[33] Beeke and Jones observed this position throughout Puritan theology as they viewed family worship as "a striking example of the Reformation doctrine of the priesthood of all believers."[34] This led to a view of family worship as divinely appointed within the home.

Wayne Grudem's commentary on 1 Peter also noted the relationship between the blessing Christians enjoy as God's chosen people and the responsibility they have in responding in worship. Although he did not apply this concept specifically to family worship, Grudem taught this truth as he examined 1 Peter 2:9: "God's purpose in redeeming us is not simply our own enjoyment but that we might glorify him."[35]

Baxter followed his initial observation with further examples. He noted seven New Testament families that were devoted to God. Crispus was presented first as he and his entire household believed in the Lord (Acts 18:8). The jailer also, along with his whole household,

---

33. Baxter, *Godly Home*, 68.
34. Beeke and Jones, *Puritan Theology*, 865.
35. Wayne A. Grudem, *Tyndale New Testament Commentaries: 1 Peter* (Downers Grove, Ill.: InterVarsity Press, 2009), 118.

believed in God (Acts 16:34). Lydia is a third example, who was baptized with the rest of her household (Acts 16:15). Baxter noted that
he does not understand this to be an example of infant baptism;
rather, only those who believed were baptized. Therefore, with each
of these, Baxter believed the reader would observe adult members of
the home laboring so that the rest of their family would also believe
and so that they may be baptized and devoted to God together.

Cornelius followed as the fourth example of one who believed
and saw his entire family set apart for the Lord (Acts 11:14). Paul also
wrote that he had baptized the household of Stephanas (1 Cor. 1:16).
Again, Baxter's position is that this serves as an example not of infant
baptism but of the head of a home with great interest and duty to see
his entire family following the Lord.

The final two examples of New Testament families set apart for
the Lord come from the life of Jesus as presented in the gospels. In
Luke 19:1–10, Jesus went to Zacchaeus's home and, following the
repentance of Zacchaeus, declared, "This day is salvation come to
this house" (Luke 19:9). Finally, Baxter noted the nobleman of John
4:53: "and himself believed, and his whole house."

Furthermore, as households are devoted to the Lord, Scripture
recognizes two pairs of relations within the home and their specific
responsibilities. First, one reads of the husband and wife. Paul wrote
that husbands are to love their wives as Christ loves the church (Eph.
5:25), and wives are to submit to their husbands (Eph. 5:22). The second pair of relations is that of parents and children. To these, Paul
called children to obey their parents (Eph. 6:1) and parents to bring
their children up in the instruction of the Lord (Eph. 6:4). So not
only the family as a whole but each specific relationship within the
home is to be sanctified to the Lord.[36]

Matthew Henry's eighteenth-century sermon included a bold
proclamation that families are societies sanctified to God. Just as the
church is a sacred society, set apart for God, so the family is to be
consecrated. Once one has surrendered himself to the Lord, he then

---

36. Baxter, *Godly Home*, 70.

surrenders all he has to Him, including his family. Henry preached, "Every good Christian that is a householder dedicates his house habitually and virtually."[37] Passages such as Genesis 28:22, Deuteronomy 20:5, and Acts 16:15 convinced Henry that families are to be sanctified and dedicated to the Lord.

Throughout Scripture, then, God is setting His people apart for His own glory, sanctifying them so that they may worship Him together. Baxter understood this as a principle that should continue today through family worship. He concluded this argument and wrote, "It is the unquestionable duty of every Christian ruler of a family to improve his interest, power, and parts to the uttermost, to bring all his family to be people of Christ in the baptismal covenant, and so to dedicate all his family to Christ.... We devote all that we have to God when we devote ourselves to him."[38]

---

37. Henry, *Church in the House*, 32.
38. Baxter, *Godly Home*, 69.

CHAPTER FOUR

Family Worship Brings Opportunities for Teaching the Word of God

As we revisit Baxter's encouragement for the family today, I hope that his first proposition has established a theological foundation for family worship. We have seen that God is worthy of this worship in the home and that families have abundant opportunities to prove faithful in this sweet discipline. Now we consider how to practically build on this theological foundation. Baxter begins by calling families to simply teach the Word of God in the home. This section examines this call in the hope that today's reader will embrace it and resolve to teach the Bible to their household.

Baxter's first proposition established that families are societies of God, devoted to Him, living in His presence, with abundant opportunities to worship Him. His second proposition built on this foundation as he wrote on the nature of this family worship, focusing on the call to teach the Word of God in the home. The second proposition is summarized as follows: "It is the will of God that the rulers of families should teach those who are under them the doctrine of salvation."[1]

As with his first proposition, Baxter afforded himself a few disclaimers. First, he noted that the heads of homes must be equipped to teach the Word of God rather than trying to teach the doctrine of salvation before they are able. He went as far as to say that, given the many opportunities to learn how to teach, it is sinful to be found unable to teach.

---

1. Baxter, *Godly Home*, 71.

Second, those teaching their families within the home are to teach according to their ability. Baxter cautioned those who, because of pride or pressure, may attempt to teach beyond their ability. His examples included those who try to interpret the original languages of Scripture without having the training or those who might try to explain obscure texts or prophecies on their own. With these cautions, Baxter simultaneously elevated the call to teach the Word of God and the care and reverence in which the Word of God is to be taught. Therefore, Baxter encouraged the heads of households to teach the plain Scriptures and most necessary doctrines that one may find in catechisms.

Finally, this family teaching is to be done in subordination to ministerial teaching. Baxter wrote, "Family teaching must give place to ministerial teaching and never be set against it."[2] It is clear that while Baxter was zealous to see every Christian family practicing family worship and teaching the Word of God in the home, he was not so desperate for it that he lowered the standard for how the Word is taught or how worship takes place in the home. He still advocated for a proper teaching and for a proper order of the church and the home.

Teaching Children the Laws of God Is One Part of Family Duty

In order to prove his position that family teaching is biblical, Baxter put forth eight biblical arguments. His intent was to prove that the Lord desires families to teach the doctrine of salvation in the home. In each of these passages, families today can see that God has provided ample opportunities for doing so.

Baxter began with three passages from Deuteronomy that command families to teach the law of God to their children. Deuteronomy 4:9, 6:7, and 11:18–21 were all offered as biblical examples of family teaching. Families are to teach the laws of God to their children when they are sitting in their homes and walking during the day, in the evenings and in the mornings. Baxter refrained from coupling these passages with any of his own commentary as he believed

---

2. Baxter, *Godly Home*, 94.

these texts demonstrate that family teaching is a duty "as plainly commanded as words can express it."[3]

Andreas Köstenberger also noted Deuteronomy 4:9 and 6:7 in his evaluation of the responsibility of teaching one's children about God and His law. He asserted that the Old Testament is "pervaded by the consciousness that parents (and especially fathers) must pass on their religious heritage to their children."[4] Köstenberger concluded that teaching God's Word in the home remains His will for Christian families today.

In Baxter's treatise *The Character of a Sound, Confirmed Christian*, the responsibility of husbands and fathers was once again addressed. Baxter drew a contrast between the strong Christian, the weak Christian, and the seeming Christian with dead faith. According to Baxter, the seeming Christian is characterized as a hypocrite who is false in his relationships with his family while pretending to be obedient to God. The weak Christian, on the other hand, is known to neglect the duty of teaching the Word of God in the home. Finally, the strong Christian father is faithful in the holy education of his children and in seeking the salvation of their souls.[5]

Baxter's sermon on Matthew 5:16 focused on ways one may glorify God. Toward the end of his sermon, Baxter preached on teaching one's children the Word of God. He taught his church that Christian parents have the responsibility to glorify God by instructing the entire family. The sermon included the bold statement that God is glorified "when parents make it their great and constant care and labor...to educate their children in the fear of God and the love of goodness and the practice of a holy life."[6]

Leland Ryken noted that Baxter is not alone in his conviction: "Puritan attitudes toward children were rooted in the conviction that

---

3. Baxter, *Godly Home*, 72.

4. Köstenberger, *God, Marriage, and Family*, 102.

5. Richard Baxter, *The Practical Works of Richard Baxter: Selected Treatises* (Peabody, Mass.: Hendrickson, 2010), 730.

6. Richard Baxter, "What Light Must Shine in Our Works?," in *Puritan Sermons, 1659–1689*, 2:485.

children belong to God and are entrusted to parents as a stewardship."[7] This responsibility is seen in other Puritan writings as well. Thomas Lye (1621–1684) preached a similar message to his congregation. He declared, "The souls of children, as well as their bodies, are committed to the care and trust of parents by the Lord, to whom they must give a strict account."[8]

Deuteronomy 6:7 also served as Matthew Henry's foundational text as he called family leaders in his congregation to teach God's commands to their children. He presented this challenge in the context of his sermon on family worship and in the immediate context of his encouragement for a family catechism. Henry preached, "You must also catechize your children…this is an excellent method of catechizing, which God himself directs us to in Deuteronomy 6:7, to teach our children the things of God, by talking of them as we sit in the house, and go by the way, when we lie down, and when we rise up."[9]

Family Teaching Includes Commanding the Laws of God

This second argument for family teaching also rests on biblical models. Both Abraham's home and Timothy's home are shown to exemplify family teaching. In Genesis 18:18–19, Abraham is chosen to "command his children and his household after him" to "keep the way of the LORD." Baxter noted that it is therefore not just a call to teach the doctrines of God but to command them with authority. Ligon Duncan and Terry Johnson also referenced Genesis 18:18–19 as one of the earliest examples of this discipline found in Scripture.[10]

Hamond also applied this passage to family worship and suggested a blessing for those who follow Abraham's example. According to Hamond, those who teach God's Word to their households "are in

---

7. Ryken, *Worldly Saints*, 78.

8. Thomas Lye, "By What Scriptural Rules May Catechizing Be So Managed, as That It May Become Most Universally Profitable?," in *Puritan Sermons, 1659–1689*, 2:180.

9. Henry, *Church in the House*, 39.

10. Ligon Duncan and Terry Johnson, "A Call to Family Worship," *Journal for Biblical Manhood and Womanhood* 9, no. 1 (Spring 2004): 7.

the most hopeful disposition to receive the communication of more light and grace to their own education and comfort."[11]

Baxter continued his argument with a New Testament example. The faithfulness of Timothy's mother and grandmother afforded him the opportunity to learn, be convinced of, and know the Scriptures from childhood (2 Tim. 1:5; 3:14–15). Matthew Henry also spoke to the importance of family teaching. He viewed the words of God as more necessary than food: "It is better to be without bread in your houses than without Bibles."[12]

Family Teaching Includes Both Instruction and Correction

Ephesians 6:4 carries the third argument: "Fathers, provoke not your children to wrath: but bring them up in the nurture and admonition of the Lord." Baxter focused on the Greek words "nurture" and "admonition," translated as "discipline" and "instruction" in several modern versions. Baxter noted that the Greek, παιδεία, translated as "discipline," is to signify "both instruction and correction, showing that parents must use both doctrine and authority with their children for the matters of the Lord."[13] This idea of family instruction is perhaps amplified with the Greek, νουθεσία, translated as "instruction" in Ephesians 6:4. Baxter wrote that this "signifies such instruction as puts doctrine into the mind and charges it on them and fully stores their minds therewith."[14] Therefore, these two words present a family teaching that finds parents correcting children with the doctrine of the Word of God and instructing them in such a way that the children store it in their own minds.

The idea of "bringing them up" in the discipline and instruction of the Lord is expressed with the Greek word ἐκτρέφετε. Baxter noted that this signifies that parents will carefully nourish their children. As

---

11. Hamond, *Case for Family Worship*, 27.
12. Henry, *Church in the House*, 36.
13. Baxter, *Godly Home*, 73.
14. Baxter, *Godly Home*, 73.

parents impart milk and food, so they will "constantly feed and nourish them with the discipline and instruction of the Lord."[15]

Baxter concluded his interaction with this verse by examining the phrase "of the Lord." He wrote, "It is called the discipline and instruction *of the Lord* because the Lord commands it and because it is the doctrine concerning the Lord, the doctrine of his teaching, and the doctrine that leads to him."[16]

Throughout Baxter's ministry, he instructed parents to teach and correct their children. He understood the danger of neglecting this ministry. It was far too common to send children into the world lacking this instruction and vulnerable in the face of temptation. He observed, "How many send their children to get sciences or trades or to travel in foreign lands before ever they were instructed at home against those temptations which they must encounter, and by which they are so often undone!"[17]

Fellow Puritan Thomas Lye also preached Ephesians 6:4 to the families of his congregation. He understood this text as proof that family teaching, including instructing children with the Word of God, must take place within the home. His sermon assumed that Christian parents will love the souls of their children. He then proclaimed, "If you love their souls indeed, your heart's desire and prayer to God for them will be that they may be saved."[18] It is this prayer, this desire, that leads Christian parents to faithfully instruct their children in obedience to Ephesians 6:4. Just as Baxter understood this aspect of family worship to be God's will, Lye concluded that it is a "necessary parental duty" to admonish one's children "to that which is truly good."[19]

---

15. Baxter, *Godly Home*, 73.

16. Baxter, *Godly Home*, 73.

17. Richard Baxter, *Dying Thoughts* (Carlisle, Pa.: Banner of Truth, 2004), 114.

18. Thomas Lye, "What May Gracious Parents Best Do for the Conversion of Those Children Whose Wickedness Is Occasioned by Their Sinful Severity or Indulgence?," in *Puritan Sermons, 1659–1689*, 3:180.

19. Lye, "What May Gracious Parents Best Do?," 3:157.

Köstenberger affirmed this position as he made the same applications of Ephesians 6:4. He examined the command for fathers to discipline and instruct their children and also applied the text to discipleship: "Fathers bear special responsibility for disciplining their children."[20] Fathers are to instruct their children in the Christian way.

As family worship includes correction, Baxter included an apologetic for discipline in the home. The nature of discipline is understood to include private reproofs, repentance, prayer, and restoration. When repentance does not take place, restoration will also be absent, and in its place will be the avoidance of the impenitent. However, Baxter was clear about his hope for discipline. He believed that both love for the soul of the one in sin and obedience to the Lord demand discipline. Furthermore, the prayer is that such discipline will lead to repentance and restoration. He wrote, "If it be possible, he may be saved from his sin, and from the power of Satan, and from the everlasting wrath of God, and may be reconciled to God and to his church."[21]

While Baxter acknowledged that family discipline is not typically referred to as worship, he offered two reasons why he considered it an act of worship. He understood it as "an authoritative act done by commission from God"[22] and as something that is to the glory of God. Therefore, he viewed family discipline as that which "should be done with as great solemnity and reverence as other parts of worship."[23] Matthew Henry also advocated for family discipline and claimed that such would allow a family to enjoy a complete church in their homes.[24]

Baxter presented Scriptures that he believed demonstrate acts of family discipline. If family worship includes teaching, and if teaching includes correction, then discipline will be a part of family worship. Baxter argued for this sort of spiritual correcting from passages such as 1 Samuel 2:22–25 and the sins of Eli's sons. Baxter wrote, "The duty of correcting…is so commonly required in Scripture, especially

---

20. Köstenberger, *God, Marriage, and Family*, 118.
21. Baxter, *Reformed Pastor*, 107.
22. Baxter, *Godly Home*, 75.
23. Baxter, *Godly Home*, 75.
24. Henry, *Church in the House*, 53.

toward children, that I will not dwell on it, lest I speak in vain what you all know already."[25] In other chapters of his directory, however, Baxter expanded in great length his thoughts of parental correcting. Discipline is to be coupled with love, as he advocated for such a great love from parents to their children that the task of correcting is well received and fruitful. Love was put forth as that which will allow children to respond to the corrective discipline of their parents. Reconciliation also takes place when correction is founded in love. Baxter wrote, "Always show them the tenderness of your love and how unwilling you are to correct them if they could be reformed any easier way; and convince them that you do it for their good."[26]

Kerry Ptacek agreed with this aspect of family discipline. Like Baxter, he noted the recurring theme woven throughout the Old Testament, particularly in the book of Proverbs. Ptacek asserted that the most common features of biblical family discipline consist of reproofs and rebukes.[27]

Richard Adams's sermon preached in the seventeenth century offered a similar proposition for family discipline. He simply observed, "If it be not too soon for children to sin, it should not be thought too soon for parents to correct."[28] Most of Adams's exhortation focused on the responsibility Christian parents have to correct their children when found in sin. Instruction is to be coupled with correction so that children may understand their folly and see the correct path. The partnership between instruction and correction also keeps in view the ultimate purpose of discipline as an act of family worship. Adams preached, "Parents are mostly concerned to get the fear of God planted in their children's tender souls, that they may know and love, trust and obey, their Maker, Redeemer, and Sanctifier."[29]

---

25. Baxter, *Godly Home*, 75.

26. Baxter, *Godly Home*, 196.

27. Ptacek, *Family Worship*, 16.

28. Richard Adams, "What Are the Duties of Parents and Children; and How Are They to Be Managed According to Scripture?," in *Puritan Sermons, 1659–1689*, 2:332.

29. Adams, "What Are the Duties of Parents and Children?," 2:333.

Michelle Anthony cited Hebrews 12:11–13 in order to lend parents a biblical model of discipline for their children. She revealed the goal of discipline as redemptive and healing while suggesting that such family discipline will always include mercy and forgiveness. Anthony concluded by stating, "Wise parents create an environment where God can work in their children's lives on this path of course correction."[30]

Family Teaching Is Seen in Proverbs 22:6

As Baxter sought to strengthen his argument that family worship includes teaching the Word of God, his fourth word of encouragement rested on Proverbs 22:6. This was the shortest of all of Baxter's arguments. In fact, no formal argument was presented. Baxter merely wrote out Proverbs 22:6: "Train up a child in the way he should go: and when he is old, he will not depart from it." Baxter declined to offer any additional application or commentary, allowing the Scripture to speak for itself and leaving the reader to assume that this verse further defends the call for family teaching.

J. I. Packer demonstrated the centrality of this text for Baxter and other Puritans: "The Puritan ethic of nurture was to train up children in the way they should go, to care for their bodies and souls together, and to educate them for sober, godly, socially useful adult living."[31]

Lye's sermon on Proverbs 22:6 also focused on application for family teaching. The command to "train up" or "catechize" was proclaimed as a prescribed duty. Parents were called to teach their children the way of life "that makes most for God's glory and his own temporal, spiritual, and eternal good."[32] Lye preached this text as he urged parents to set their children apart for dedication to the Lord. While the phrase "and when he is old, he will not depart from it" was

---

30. Michelle D. Anthony, "Equipping Parents to Be the Spiritual Leaders in the Home," in *A Theology for Family Ministries*, ed. Michael Anthony and Michelle Anthony (Nashville, Tenn.: B&H Academic, 2011), 200.

31. Packer, *Quest for Godliness*, 25.

32. Thomas Lye, "By What Scriptural Rules?," in *Puritan Sermons, 1659–1689*, 2:99.

not preached as a promise, Lye did encourage the church that it does mean a child would "be the better for it as long as he lives."[33] The sermon concluded with an observation on the clarity with which the Scriptures command this sort of family teaching: "How deeply parents are obliged to this duty, is written, as it were with a sun-beam, in the Scriptures, where we find precepts, precedents, arguments, more than many, to evince it."[34]

Köstenberger made a similar application of Proverbs 22:6. He too understood that this text does not guarantee certain results, as children will decide whether to follow the Lord. However, Köstenberger suggested that children tend to follow what they were taught. For this reason, "parental discipline and instruction are so important."[35] The family teaching and instruction in view throughout the book of Proverbs carries both positive and negative teachings. In Proverbs, Köstenberger observed twenty-one positive attributes that parents are to teach their children. These include justice, kindness, generosity, prudence, contentment, humility, faithfulness, and purity. Likewise, there are a number of Proverbs that call parents to teach their children to avoid other attributes. These negative teachings find parents warning their children of seeking pleasure, gluttony, arrogance, and vanity.[36]

Children Are Charged to Obey, Implying a Charge for Family Teaching

As Baxter continued to encourage families to teach the Word of God in the home, he approached his fifth argument, not from the role of the parents as seen in Ephesians 6:4 but from the responsibility of children. He briefly mentioned four Scriptures that charge children to hear, obey, and not forsake the teaching of their parents (Deut. 21:18–21; Prov. 1:8; 6:20; 23:22). Such a charge assumes that

---

33. Lye, "What May Gracious Parents Best Do?," 3:100.
34. Lye, "What May Gracious Parents Best Do?," 3:105.
35. Köstenberger, *God, Marriage, and Family*, 103.
36. Köstenberger, *God, Marriage, and Family*, 104–5.

family teaching is taking place. Therefore, the fact that children are expected to obey the teaching of their parents implies that parents are to be teaching their children.

Another Puritan preacher, Richard Adams (ca. 1626–1698), delivered a sermon on the duties of children to their parents and the duties of parents to their children. Adams began with the biblical responsibility children have to obey their parents. Like Baxter, Adams believed that this obligation implies that parents are expected to teach something that children are to obey. Christian parents are reminded of their charge to watch over the souls of their children by teaching the Word of God diligently. Adams called parents to be "solicitous to get the seeds sown in their tender hearts, before the weeds of the world grow-up therein and canker the soil."[37]

Husbands Are to Teach Their Wives for Their Instruction and Sanctification

Thus far, Baxter's arguments for family teaching focused primarily on parents teaching their children. His sixth argument, however, shifted to an emphasis on the call for husbands to teach their wives. First Peter 3:7 was written out with no commentary. Baxter seemed to link it to Ephesians 5:25–26, but he never explained how the call for husbands to live with their wives in an understanding way can be understood as a call to teach their wives.

Ptacek exposited the Ephesians 5 text to explain that husbands are to play a role in the sanctification of their wives. He advocated for an interpretation of verse 26, "that he might sanctify and cleanse it with the washing of water by the word," that finds husbands spiritually nurturing their wives. He wrote, "The husband's role in the sanctification of his wife must involve the use of the Bible."[38]

---

37. Adams, "What Are the Duties of Parents?," 2:335.
38. Ptacek, *Family Worship*, 33.

Donald Whitney expanded on 1 Peter 3:7 and its application to family worship. He wrote, "Have you realized that the prayers here are those prayed together by husbands and wives? Peter assumes that Christian couples pray together."[39]

Baxter did provide an explanation for Ephesians 5:25–26: "This plainly implies that this knowledge must be used for the instruction and sanctification of the wife."[40] Just as Jesus cleansed His bride "by the washing of water with the word," husbands are to sanctify their wives by instructing them with the Word of God. Whitney also relates this passage to family worship. He wrote, "One of the best ways that husbands can bring the pure water of the Word of God into their homes is through the spiritually cleansing and refreshing practice of family worship."[41]

First Corinthians 14:34–35 concludes Baxter's sixth argument. He did not acknowledge any controversy surrounding this passage, as is often seen in today's church; rather, he plainly and simply gave application from the end of the passage that reads, "Let them ask their husbands at home." Rather than focusing on the limitations of a woman's role in the church, Baxter elevated the husband's role in the home. He wrote, "This shows that at home their husbands must teach them."[42]

Another Puritan pastor, Richard Steele (1629–1692), also preached on the duties husbands have toward their wives, as he expounded on Ephesians 5 throughout his sermon. He began with the chief duty of every husband to love his wife. Steele then expanded on this meaning to include the particular responsibility of "diligent instruction of his wife."[43] As Steele, Baxter, and other Puritans wrote on spiritual leadership in marriage, emphasis was given to the responsibility of the husband to teach his wife the Word of

---

39. Donald S. Whitney, *Family Worship* (Wheaton, Ill.: Crossway, 2016), 26.
40. Baxter, *Godly Home*, 74.
41. Whitney, *Family Worship*, 24.
42. Baxter, *Godly Home*, 74.
43. Richard Steele, "What Are the Duties of Husbands and Wives towards Each Other?," in *Puritan Sermons, 1659–1689*, 2:286.

God. Ryken observed, "The husband's headship, according to the Puritans, is not a ticket to privilege but a charge to responsibility."[44]

Scripture Commands Believers to Teach One Another

Baxter's support of family worship was not limited to biblical passages that explicitly referenced families, households, spouses, or children. Scriptures that speak to the relationship between believers (the "one anothers") were also applied to the home. For example, Baxter read Colossians 3:16 and the command to "let the word of Christ dwell in you richly in all wisdom; teaching and admonishing one another," and he wrote, "and much more must a man do to wife and children than to those more remote."[45]

In other words, if a man is called to teach the Word of Christ to those outside the house, then it is assumed that he is first called to teach the Word to those inside the house. In the same way, the command to exhort one another, found in Hebrews 3:13, was followed with Baxter's comment, "Much more must the rulers of families do to wives, children, and servants."[46]

Ptacek examined many Scriptures to evaluate the claim that family worship should include teaching. He followed Baxter's lead in declaring that Scripture does indeed command Christians to teach the Word of God in the home. He specifically noted Psalm 78 as a reminder of this responsibility. For Ptacek, the options are simple: "A father has two options: either he teaches his children about God's dealings with his people or he hides them from his children. There is no neutral ground for the believing father."[47]

Like Ptacek, Michelle Anthony also invoked Psalm 78:2–7 as a clear reminder that God has chosen to "use the family as the primary place to nurture faith."[48] Anthony made two applications for today's church. First, she exhorted parents to act as the spiritual leaders of

---

44. Ryken, *Worldly Saints*, 75–76.
45. Baxter, *Godly Home*, 74.
46. Baxter, *Godly Home*, 74.
47. Ptacek, *Family Worship*, 15.
48. Anthony, "Equipping Parents," 183.

the home. Second, she challenged the church to equip parents for this calling.

Church Leaders Are to Manage Their Own Households

Baxter had already addressed children, parents, and spouses. In his final encouragement of family teaching as an aspect of household worship, Baxter addressed church leaders.

Paul taught Timothy that an overseer must be one that "ruleth well his own house, having his children in subjection with all gravity; (For if a man know not how to rule his own house, how shall he take care of the church of God?)" (1 Tim. 3:4–5). Paul made a similar statement about those who would serve as deacons: "Let the deacons be the husbands of one wife, ruling their children and their own houses well" (1 Tim. 3:12). These two passages drive Baxter's final argument.

He offered two main observations. First, he believed that since overseers and deacons are to have demonstrated these virtues before being asked to serve, the call to manage one's household is for all Christians. Second, the call to manage one's household is compared to managing the church. Since management of the church is a holy governing "in the things of God and salvation," then the same sort of holy governing in the doctrine of God is meant for the home.[49]

This holy governing is seen in Joel Beeke's writings as well. Beeke seemed to follow Baxter's position as he challenged men to manage their households as spiritual leaders. Faithful management will find leaders teaching their children, interceding for their household, and, most notably, leading through family worship. Beeke wrote, "Daily family worship ought to be the foundation of your fatherly exercising of your prophetical office toward your children."[50]

---

49. Baxter, *Godly Home*, 74.

50. Joel R. Beeke, *How Should Men Lead Their Families?* (Grand Rapids: Reformation Heritage, 2014), 6. See also James W. Alexander, *Thoughts on Family Worship* (Tomball, Tex.: Legacy Ministry Publications, 2010). Alexander, an American Presbyterian minister of the nineteenth century, argued that family worship is a duty and responsibility. Like Baxter, Alexander elevated the importance of managing one's household and leading one's family. He considered the heads of homes to be bound to watch for the souls of their family members.

༄

CHAPTER FIVE

Family Worship Fills the
Home with Prayer and Praises

Baxter's theology of family worship provides a biblical picture of families enjoying abundant opportunities to worship together and teach the Word of God in the home. His last proposition further builds on this foundation as Baxter concentrates on two additional aspects of family worship: solemn prayer and praises of God. As with the previous encouragement for family teaching, the call to prayer and praises remains a practical point of application. Families today hoping to cultivate worship in their home may find these final points extremely accessible.

Baxter challenged the reader to observe two things. First, all of the previous arguments have proven that family worship is God's will. Second, worship throughout Scripture includes prayer and praise, so family worship will fill the home with the same. Baxter therefore put forth many of these Scriptures in the following twenty arguments to prove that just as family worship includes teaching, it also includes prayer and praises.

Elements of Family Worship

Baxter not only advocated for family worship but also taught its elements, including teaching the Word of God, discipline, and prayer and praises. These elements prove common throughout many writings on family worship.

Matthew Henry's preaching called his church to allow the Word of God to be at the center of their family worship. He exhorted them as he preached, "Let me therefore with all earnestness press it upon you to make the solemn reading of the Scripture a part of your daily worship in your families."[1] Families were challenged to read through the entire Bible while also devoting attention to catechizing their children. Even with this emphasis on the Word of God, Henry, like Baxter, also noted the importance of singing praises as a necessary element for family worship.

In the nineteenth century, William Plumer shared his own list of disciplines that constitute family worship. He included Bible study, praises, and prayer. The praises should be sung when possible and read as a hymn when singing is not an option. The prayers included those of "adoration, thanksgiving, confession, and supplication."[2]

Donald Whitney proposed a similar recipe. He called families to enjoy reading the Word of God together while also praying and singing with one another. He added that, if time permits, catechisms and Scripture memorization should also receive consideration.[3]

Ligon Duncan and Terry Johnson highlighted three elements of family worship based on the foundation of Scripture. For them, worship in the home consists of reading Scripture, singing Scripture, and praying Scripture: "In these settings great psalms and hymns are sung, children are catechized, sins are confessed, and the Scriptures are read and taught."[4]

Ptacek's list of family worship elements proves similar. He examined Ephesians 5:19–20 and Colossians 3:16 to arrive at his order of family worship, advocating for the inclusion of "instruction, praises, prayer, and discipline."[5]

Praises and prayer remained the focus of Baxter's final proposition. He spent more time on these elements than any others. Such emphasis is seen in the number of arguments presented, the length

---

1. Henry, *Church in the House*, 37.

2. William S. Plumer, "The Lord's Day at Home," in Pollard and Brown, *Theology of the Family*, 736.

3. Whitney, *Family Worship*, 46–49.

4. Duncan and Johnson, "Call to Family Worship," 15.

5. Ptacek, *Family Worship*, 30.

devoted to this subject in his *Christian Directory*, and the number of Scriptures offered to the reader.

Christian Families Have Opportunities for Prayer and Praise

Baxter began his apologetic by examining the occasions and opportunities Christian families have to pray and praise, for if such opportunities exist, then the Lord desires that Christians improve on or take advantage of them. When this is done, prayer and praise will fill the home. The first six Scriptures presented are meant as an encouragement to do so.

First Timothy 2:8 reads, "I will therefore that men pray every where." To this Baxter responded, "If men must pray everywhere, then for certain in their families."[6] The same sort of application was made to 1 Thessalonians 5:17–18 and the command to "pray without ceasing." Baxter simply noted that Christians are not to cease praying when they are with their families. As Colossians 4:2 calls believers to continue in prayer with thanksgiving, and Colossians 3:17 calls the same to give thanks to God, then, as Baxter noted, surely Christian families will be found praying and giving thanks to the Lord together for the mercies they have received: "If men must continue in prayer and watch in it and in thanksgiving, then doubtless they must not omit the singular advantages that are administered in families."[7]

The final two Scriptures in this section are Romans 12:12 and Ephesians 6:18–19. Here the reader is reminded of the commands for "continuing instant in prayer" and "praying always with all prayer and supplication in the Spirit." Baxter recognized that some might disagree with his application, offering the objection "But this binds us no more to prayer in our families than anywhere else."[8] To this sort of objection Baxter responded, "It binds us to take all fit

---

6. Baxter, *Godly Home*, 76.
7. Baxter, *Godly Home*, 76.
8. Baxter, *Godly Home*, 76.

opportunities; and we have more fit opportunities in our own families" than in other meetings, "except the church."[9]

Furthermore, Baxter rejected the notion that Scripture must specifically mention family prayer before one begins praying with the family. Instead, he advocated that general biblical commands for prayer remain a sufficient defense for family prayer. He again referenced Ephesians 6:18 and the command to pray at all times. Although this verse does not outline specific places or times for prayer, Baxter interpreted "all times" as a call to not "omit fit advantages and opportunities for prayer."[10] He concluded, "So if God bids you to pray in all places and at all times, on all occasions (that are fit for prayer), and experience and common reason tell you that families afford the most fit times, places, and occasions for prayer, is it not enough that there are such seasons, opportunities, and occasions for family prayer?"[11]

While these passages do not specifically define the frequency of family worship and prayer, Baxter provided eight arguments for his view that these should be practiced every day. He also supported the view that family worship should take place twice a day, every day, with morning and evening presented as the fittest seasons.[12]

First, Baxter pointed to the daily needs of every family. Families sin and receive mercy daily. They also need provision, protection, direction, and blessings daily. Each day finds every family needing to spend time confessing sins and seeking supplication. Therefore, they have reason to pray, worship, and give thanks every day.[13]

Second, the Lord's Prayer is presented as clear direction to pray daily. Baxter wrote, "The Lord's Prayer directs us daily to put up such prayers as belong to families." In the prayer "Give us this day our daily bread," he points out that the plural *us* obliges families to pray for their daily bread together.[14] Levin Schücking invoked the history

---

9. Baxter, *Godly Home*, 76.
10. Baxter, *Godly Home*, 77.
11. Baxter, *Godly Home*, 77.
12. Baxter, *Godly Home*, 94.
13. Baxter, *Godly Home*, 94.
14. Baxter, *Godly Home*, 95.

of Puritan family worship practices when he wrote, "At every meal, both at midday and in the evening, someone should recite in a loud voice the different sentences of the Lord's Prayer."[15]

The third observation rests on passages such as 1 Thessalonians 5:17–18, "Pray without ceasing. In every thing give thanks"; Colossians 4:1–2, which presents a call to "continue in prayer"; and Philippians 4:6, which reminds readers that "in every thing by prayer and supplication with thanksgiving" they are to let their "requests be made known unto God." Baxter engaged these three texts to convince families that "it is easy to see that less than twice a day does not fulfill the command to pray without ceasing, steadfastly, and in everything. The phrases seem to go much higher."[16] Hamond presented this same argument, also pointing to Philippians 4:6. He taught that this passage implied more than morning and evening prayer for family worship. Hamond went so far as to claim that morning and evening family worship is indeed a duty for Christians.[17]

Baxter's fourth point is similar to his third. He briefly referenced Daniel's practice of praying in his house three times a day. Baxter then concluded that, in light of this example from Scripture, praying together in the house less than twice a day would be unreasonable.[18]

First Timothy 5:5 supports the fifth observation. As Paul wrote about the widow who "continueth in supplications and prayers night and day," Baxter applied this Scripture to his teaching on the frequency of family worship, stating, "Night and day can be no less than morning and evening."[19] He then anticipated the reader's objection by writing, "If you say, 'this is not family prayer,' I answer that it is all kinds of prayer belonging to her, and if it commends the less, so much more the greater."[20]

---

15. Levin L. Schücking, *The Puritan Family: A Social Study from the Literary Sources* (New York: Schocken Books, 1970), 61.

16. Baxter, *Godly Home*, 95.

17. Hamond, *Case for Family Worship*, 110–11.

18. Baxter, *Godly Home*, 95.

19. Baxter, *Godly Home*, 95.

20. Baxter, *Godly Home*, 95.

The sixth point cites eleven Old and New Testament passages: Joshua 1:8; Nehemiah 1:6; Psalm 1:2; 88:1; Luke 2:37; 6:12; 18:7; Acts 26:7; 1 Thessalonians 3:10; 2 Timothy 1:3; and Revelation 7:15. In each of these, Baxter found examples of either Jesus Christ or God's people praying, meditating on Scripture, or reading Scripture night and day.[21]

The final two observations reference Old Testament Scriptures. Deuteronomy 6:7 and 11:19 support Baxter's seventh point. Both passages command parents to teach their children when they rise (morning) and when they lie down (evening). Little commentary was added. Baxter merely noted these passages as further proof that family worship should take place twice daily. Leon M. Blanchette unpacked the implication of these passages, writing, "Teaching obedience to God's commands is to be done at all times, in all places, with intention, as parents are being obedient to God's commands."[22]

Baxter's final observation on the frequency of family prayer began with Psalm 119:164 and David's statement that he praised God seven times a day. Baxter then moved on to several other psalms that illustrate a pattern of prayer or praise in the morning (these include Pss. 5:3; 59:16; 88:13; and 119:147–148). The argument is simple: David prayed in the morning, the priests offered sacrifices and thanksgiving to the Lord every morning (Ex. 30:7; Lev. 6:12; 1 Chron. 23:30; 2 Chron. 13:11; Ezek. 46:13–14; Amos 4:4), and therefore Christians, the holy priesthood, are to offer worship to the Lord morning and evening. Baxter commented, "All these show how frequently God's servants have been accustomed to worship him and how often God expects it."[23]

Family prayer appears to be common throughout church history. For example, second-century Christians would enjoy their first family prayer upon the birth of a child. In this case, children experienced family prayer from the day they were born. This first family prayer

---

21. Baxter, *Godly Home*, 95.

22. Leon M. Blanchette Jr., "Spiritual Markers in the Life of a Child," in *A Theology for Family Ministries* (Nashville, Tenn.: B&H Academic, 2011), 121–22.

23. Baxter, *Godly Home*, 95–96.

expressed "gratitude for receiving the child from God's hands."[24] Clement of Alexandria and Cyprian both referenced family prayers that included children. Chrysostom called parents to pray with their children each evening, leaning on the psalms as a guide.[25] Examples from both Scripture and early church life strengthen Baxter's view that Christian families have opportunities for praying together.

Family Needs and Blessings Necessitate Family Prayer

Every family has needs, and every family receives blessings from God. Therefore, they must come together to pray both for their needs and for giving praise and thanksgiving for the blessings the Lord has provided. As Henry preached, "All family blessings are owing to Christ, and come to us through his hand and by his blood.... Shall not the God of your mercies, your family mercies, be the God of your praises, your family praises, and that daily?"[26]

Baxter anticipated the objection that individual family members could simply pray for these needs and thank God for this provision on their own. He reminded the reader that families share many needs together and should, therefore, pray together. These needs shared by all in the home include the well-being of the household, the preservation and direction of the family, and the provision of the family. Henry agreed: "Daily bread is received by families together, and we are taught not only to pray for it every day, but to pray together for it."[27]

One of Thomas Doolittle's seven reasons families should pray focused on the needs within the home. Like Baxter, he assumed that as families share needs, they share prayers for provision for those needs. To neglect such prayers would communicate that the family is living on their own strength without recognizing their dependence on God. A family's acknowledgment of their needs and of their

---

24. Cornelia B. Horn and John W. Martens, *Let the Little Children Come to Me: Childhood and Children in Early Christianity* (Washington, D.C.: Catholic University of America Press, 2009), 294–95.

25. Horn and Martens, *Let the Little Children Come to Me*, 295.

26. Henry, *Church in the House*, 45, 48–49.

27. Henry, *Church in the House*, 49.

dependence on the Lord for those needs will lead them to their knees in prayer together.[28]

God Has Given Charge to the Head of the Home to Lead in Worship

The head of the home has received a charge from the Lord to see that the rest of the family comes together for worship. Leading in worship is also understood here as a responsibility to equip the rest of the family to be able to pray and worship. This is to be done together as a whole rather than one-on-one. This was Baxter's position that he defended with three Old Testament examples.

The first comes from the Ten Commandments. The fourth commandment is not just a command for each individual to remember the Sabbath and keep it holy (Ex. 20:8). Verse ten reads, "In it thou shalt not do any work, thou, nor thy son, nor thy daughter, thy manservant, nor thy maidservant, nor thy cattle, nor thy stranger that is within thy gates." Baxter noted that this command requires the head of the home to make sure that all in his household sanctify the Sabbath.

Baxter expanded on this notion in his catechism for families. He offered thirty-nine questions and answers surrounding the fourth commandment. The thirty-third question inquires of the private duties of the Lord's Day. Baxter's response called families to spend the day singing praises to God, catechizing their households, meditating on Scripture, and praying together.[29] George Hamond also understood the fourth commandment to lend insight into family worship: "Let experience be heard to testify, whether family worship and the sanctification of the Sabbath do not ordinarily thrive or decline together."[30]

Second, Baxter referred to the Abrahamic covenant of circumcision. He viewed this as yet another reference to the head of the

---

28. Thomas Doolittle, "Seven Reasons Families Should Pray," in Pollard and Brown, *Theology of the Family*, 76–77.

29. Richard Baxter, *A Puritan Catechism for Families* (Bellingham, Wash.: Lexham Press, 2017), 240.

30. Hamond, *Case for Family Worship*, 100.

home's responsibility to lead the entire family in that which honors the Lord. The same may be seen in Exodus 12:2–3 as the Passover was observed by the entire family and the sacrifice was according to each household. Baxter concluded with his third example as he noted the same application of the Feast of Weeks.[31]

In Daniel Doriani's examining the Puritan view of headship within the home, Baxter's view was presented as the prevailing Puritan position. Doriani noted that the head of the household remained responsible for the spiritual formation of the family. This God-given duty was a right and responsibility that was not to be delegated to anyone else, and family worship was considered the chief responsibility.[32]

Andreas Köstenberger also affirmed the husband as the head of the family, pointing to Ephesians 5:23: "For the husband is the head of the wife, even as Christ is the head of the church: and he is the saviour of the body." According to Köstenberger, this text affirms the husband's headship within the home.[33] This headship is a responsibility that fathers should not abdicate to anyone else. Instead, "as the head of the home, the father ought to assume responsibility for leading his children to Christ and of encouraging them on the path of Christian discipleship."[34] Vern Poythress has also explored the parallels between the church and the home, focusing in particular on the relationship between leadership in the church and leadership in the home. Poythress referenced Ephesians 5–6 as he asserted, "The leadership within a family is vested in the husband and father."[35]

---

31. Baxter, *Godly Home*, 79.

32. Daniel Doriani, "The Godly Household in Puritan Theology, 1560–1640," (PhD diss., Westminster Theological Seminary, 1986), 72–74.

33. Köstenberger, *God, Marriage, and Family*, 68.

34. Köstenberger, *God, Marriage, and Family*, 171.

35. Vern Sheridan Poythress, "The Church as Family: Why Male Leadership in the Family Requires Male Leadership in the Church," in *Recovering Biblical Manhood and Womanhood*, ed. John Piper and Wayne Grudem (Wheaton, Ill.: Crossway, 2012), 237–38.

Christian Families Should Prefer Joint Prayer and Praises

Baxter suggested that God prefers the prayers and praises of many Christians together and that Christian families also ought to prefer the same.[36] As with many of his previous arguments, Baxter presented a handful of biblical texts to defend his argument. He began with Colossians 3:16 as a reminder that there is a call to praise God together and not just individually. In the same way, Acts 12:12 shows a group of believers praying together. Baxter wrote, "They judged it better to pray together than alone."[37] This is also seen in Acts 20:36 when Paul prayed with the Ephesian elders.

The fourth passage presented comes from James 5:14 and the command for the sick to "call for the elders of the church; and let them pray over him." Once again, corporate prayer is encouraged in the Scriptures. Baxter also noted that Hebrews 10:25 encourages believers to meet together. He saw in this verse an emphasis on church prayer over private prayer, which he also observed in Paul's plea in Romans 15:30: "Strive together with me in your prayers."

Although Baxter acknowledged the value and importance of private or secret prayer, he continued to present biblical examples of corporate prayer. All of this is put forth in support of his premise that Christian families should prefer joint prayer. He quoted Matthew 18:20 without presenting context or commentary before moving back to the book of Acts. The church came together in one accord and devoted themselves to prayer in Acts 1:14 and 1:24. Baxter then concluded by noting that when Jesus taught His disciples to pray in Matthew 6:9–13, He used the plural "*Our* Father," "Give *us* this day," and so on.[38] Baxter rested on this as evidence that God expects joint prayer.

Thomas Doolittle advocated for joint prayer within the home based on the observable truth that families jointly enjoy mercies from God daily. He therefore argued they should come together

---

36. Baxter, *Godly Home*, 79.
37. Baxter, *Godly Home*, 80.
38. Baxter, *Godly Home*, 80.

daily to praise God for such mercies: "You should not quietly sleep till you have been together on your knees."[39]

Christian Families Have a Duty to Receive All the Mercies That God Offers

Baxter's approach is a little different here. He did not offer any passages as a positive command to receive God's mercies. Instead, he presented two passages that warn against refusing God's mercies. Proverbs 1:24 and Matthew 23:37 are held up to teach that "to refuse an offered kindness is contempt and ingratitude."[40] Baxter assumed the reader would agree that the opportunity for a family to come together in prayer is indeed a mercy from God. With these two biblical warnings, he hoped then to have convinced the reader to receive this mercy by coming together in joint prayers and praises.

The mercies of God also advance Hamond's argument for family worship, which appeals to Hebrews 4:16: "Let us therefore come boldly unto the throne of grace, that we may obtain mercy, and find grace to help in time of need." Since families need mercy every day, and in light of the biblical call to draw near in order to receive mercy, there remains an opportunity to receive it together through family worship.[41]

Some Family Duties Are Diminished If Not Performed Jointly

Two family duties mentioned here are singing praises and teaching. Baxter suggested that these may lose their excellency if not done jointly. It is clear that teaching the Word of God cannot be done alone, for there must be one who is teaching and one who is being taught. Singing praises is also presented as a family duty that is enriched when done jointly, for then there may be harmony. No Scripture was presented in support of this position.

---

39. Doolittle, "Seven Reasons Families Should Pray," 75.
40. Baxter, *Godly Home*, 81.
41. Hamond, *Case for Family Worship*, 111.

William Plumer also assumed that certain duties are expected to be done jointly in the home. These duties included both prayer and praises. He wrote, "Every family has wants, which should lead it to unite in prayer. Every family has mercies, which demand a united song."[42]

Inclinations for Family Prayer and Praises Are from the Spirit of God

Baxter assumed from experience that unless a Christian is battling sin or temptation, they will have an inclination toward family prayer and praise. He believed that the Spirit of God impresses a love for these duties on the hearts of believers. Without providing any specific Scripture references, Baxter argued that such inclinations for family prayer and praises are from the Holy Spirit. It was said to be demonstrated in the fact that such inclinations come upon the heart at the same time as all other grace and by the same means. Family worship, then, must be from the Spirit, who preserves such an inclination and causes it to increase. As Baxter preached, "God must be worshipped as a Spirit in spirit and truth."[43] Family prayer and praises are "so agreeable to the Word that a Christian sins against his new nature when he neglects family duties."[44] Baxter therefore concluded, "God by his Spirit, creates a desire after them and an estimation of them in every gracious soul."[45]

The relationship between family prayer and the Spirit of God seems consistent with the Puritan thought of Baxter's time. Beeke's research acknowledged this connection, noting that the Puritan had "a sense of dependency on the Holy Spirit coupled with a life of prayerfulness."[46] Wayne Grudem highlighted this dependency well: "Apart from the work of the Spirit of God, a person will not receive

---

42. Plumer, "Lord's Day at Home," 738.

43. Richard Baxter, "What Light Must Shine in Our Works?," in *Puritan Sermons, 1659–1689*, 2:476.

44. Baxter, *Godly Home*, 82.

45. Baxter, *Godly Home*, 82–83.

46. Beeke, *Puritan Evangelism*, 71.

spiritual truths and in particular will not receive or accept the truth that the words of Scripture are in fact the words of God."[47]

Family Prayer and Praises Bring Blessings on the Home

Experience rather than Scripture carries Baxter's eighth argument, in which he noted that joint prayer and praise will benefit and bless the family. He challenged the reader to compare the families they know who pray and praise together with the families they know who do not. Baxter expected that those who do not practice such family worship will be more likely to abound with worldliness, while those who practice family worship will abound with "faith, patience, temperance, charity, and repentance."[48]

Centuries after Baxter's ministry, Arthur Pink also wrote on the blessings that families enjoy through joint praise and prayer. After he considered the biblical examples of Abraham and Joshua, Pink turned his attention to his readers and their own practice of family worship: "If we would enjoy the blessing of God upon our family, then let its members gather together daily for praise and prayer."[49] He concluded, "Family prayer gains for us the presence and blessing of the Lord."[50]

A Christian Family Is a Church

Baxter introduced the major idea that "all churches ought solemnly to pray to God and praise him."[51] He did not seek to prove this idea but rather focused on his minor idea, "A Christian family is a church,"[52] which would then prove that Christian families ought solemnly to pray to God and praise Him. Baxter defined the nature of a

---

47. Wayne Grudem, *Systematic Theology: An Introduction to Biblical Doctrine* (Grand Rapids: Zondervan, 1994), 77.

48. Baxter, *Godly Home*, 83.

49. Arthur W. Pink, "Family Worship," in Pollard and Brown, *Theology of the Family*, 49.

50. Pink, "Family Worship," 51.

51. Baxter, *Godly Home*, 83.

52. Baxter, *Godly Home*, 83.

church as "a society of Christians gathered for the worshipping and serving of God."[53] Since a Christian family is also a society of God, consisting of Christians who gather together and worship Him, it may be understood as a church that ought to pray and praise. Baxter did draw a distinction between a Christian family praying and praising as a church in the home and the organized church that consists of many families. He conceded that the two are of different species, although he did not identify the differences.

Baxter's lack of clarity on this distinction proves problematic as many challenge the idea that a Christian family is a church. Some of the marks of a church are often missing in a Christian home, even when family worship is consistent. R. C. Sproul highlighted three distinctive characteristics of a valid church. He asserted that these three characteristics were championed by many of the Protestant Reformers as well. These marks include faithful gospel preaching, the administration of the sacraments (the Lord's Supper and baptism), and church discipline.[54] Since Baxter did not advocate for the inclusion of the sacraments in family worship, it seems that a Christian family practicing family worship would not constitute as a church in and of itself.

However, Baxter claimed that Scripture expresses the idea that a Christian family is a church, citing four passages to support his argument.[55] He quoted 1 Corinthians 16:19, noting Aquila and Prisca and "the church that is in their house." Philemon 2 also mentions the church in a home, as does Romans 16:5 and Colossians 4:15. In one of his sermons, Baxter preached that it glorified and honored God "when the houses of Christians are societies of saints and churches of God, and live in love and concord together."[56] Baxter recognized

---

53. Baxter, *Godly Home*, 83.

54. R. C. Sproul, *What Is the Church?* (Orlando: Reformation Trust, 2013), 62–63.

55. In his dissertation, Daniel Doriani presented the Puritan idea of the home and its relationship to the church: "Both are societies ordained by God in which the worship of God is of paramount importance." Daniel Doriani, "The Godly Household in Puritan Theology," 53.

56. Baxter, "What Light Must Shine?," 486.

that some offer a different interpretation of these passages as they understand this to refer to churches that would meet or assemble in these homes rather than families acting as a church.

This alternative interpretation continues to receive support today. Douglas Moo offered this position in his commentary on the book of Romans. He engaged the debate regarding Paul's greeting to Prisca and Aquila in Romans 16:5 and "the church that is in their house." Moo recognized that this could be a reference to "the church made up of members of their household."[57] This was Baxter's understanding. However, Moo concluded that this is an unlikely meaning of the text, writing, "This means the church that meets in their house…the house church."[58]

Moo offered the same interpretation for the Colossians 4:15 reference. Although Baxter pointed to this passage as an example of a family living as a church in their household, Moo disagreed with this explanation. Moo viewed the church in Nymphas's home as a house church. This would include more than just Nymphas's family. According to Moo, it is likely that Nymphas supported the rest of the church by allowing them to meet and worship in his home.[59] He provided the same conclusion for Philemon 2. In this case, Moo considered the phrase "the church in your house" as a reference to "a congregation of Christians meeting in a particular home."[60] Likewise, Stephen Um interpreted 1 Corinthians 16:19, one of Baxter's foundational verses for his argument, as nothing more than a greeting from a house church.[61]

George Hamond, on the other hand, joined Baxter in making his case for family worship, in part, based on these Scriptures and the

---

57. Douglas J. Moo, *The New International Commentary on the New Testament: The Epistle to the Romans* (Grand Rapids: Eerdmans, 1996), 920.

58. Moo, *Epistle to the Romans*, 920.

59. Douglas J. Moo, *The Pillar New Testament Commentary: The Letters to the Colossians and to Philemon* (Grand Rapids: Eerdmans, 2008), 349.

60. Moo, *Letters to the Colossians and to Philemon*, 383.

61. Stephen T. Um, *Preaching the Word: 1 Corinthians, the Word of the Cross* (Wheaton, Ill.: Crossway, 2015), 298.

idea that a Christian family is a church. Referencing Romans 16:5, Hamond wrote, "It is fitting that all the families of the faithful should be so ordered that they may be as so many little churches."[62] Like Baxter, Hamond also leaned on 1 Corinthians 16:19, Philemon 2, and Colossians 4:15 as further evidence for his argument. Hamond believed that Paul's mention of "Nymphas and the church in his house" (Col. 4:15) afforded the church a description of one family that should be true of all Christian families.

Hamond suggested that if these references do indeed allude to domestic churches, then his case for family worship has been made. If the Christian family is a church, then family worship must exist, for it would not be a true church if worship were absent.[63] Hamond did concede that others may interpret these passages as examples of church congregations meeting in the home rather than the family meeting as a church in their own home. He specifically attributed this viewpoint to Joseph Mede (1586–1639).[64]

Joseph Mede first published his position in 1638 in *Churches, That Is, Appropriate Places for Christian Worship Both in, and Ever since the Apostles Times*. In this work Mede quoted the same passages that Baxter and Hamond referenced, but he offered a different interpretation. Concerning these passages, Mede wrote, "Which I understand not, to be spoken of their families as it is commonly expounded, but of the congregation of the Saints, there wont to assemble for the performance of divine duties."[65] He argued that there must have been something unique about the gatherings in these homes since Paul singles them out. If these references are nothing more than greetings

62. Hamond, *Case for Family Worship*, 84.

63. Jody Anderson's 2009 dissertation addressed Baxter and Hamond's interpretation: "While the interpretation that sees house churches as family churches emerges from eisegesis, the emphasis employed by Hamond and…Baxter…remains valid for the issue of family worship." Anderson, "Church within the Church," 128.

64. Hamond, *Case for Family Worship*, 85.

65. Joseph Mede, *Churches, That Is, Appropriate Places for Christian Worship Both in, and Ever since the Apostles Times. A Discourse at First More Briefly Delivered in a College Chapel, and Since Enlarged*, Oxford Text Archive, p. 25, http://ota.ox.ac.uk/id/A07381.

to a family who, by nature of their practice of family worship, are considered a church, then it would suggest that they were the only ones faithful in their family worship since they are the only ones who receive such a description. Instead, Mede concluded that Paul is greeting church congregations that were meeting in the homes of the named believers.

Kerry Ptacek more recently examined these same passages to reach the same conclusion. He too taught that these New Testament passages refer to house churches. For example, he pointed to Nymphas in Colossians 4:15 as one who simply had a house large enough for the entire congregation to meet. Ptacek drew the same interpretation from 1 Corinthians 16:19 and Romans 16:5. However, Ptacek informed the reader that Matthew Henry, along with others, see in these passages examples of families enjoying worship in the home as a church.[66]

On April 16, 1704, Matthew Henry (1662–1714) preached a sermon based on the 1 Corinthians 16:19 text. His sermon clearly disagreed with Mede's position and, instead, sided with Hamond and Baxter. Henry began his sermon by recognizing positions like Mede's. He knew that some interpreted 1 Corinthians 16:19 as a reference to a meeting of many Christians in Aquila and Priscilla's house rather than to a family worshiping together as a church. Henry then followed Baxter and Hamond by introducing the other three passages: Romans 16:5, Colossians 4:15, and Philemon 2. The lesson that Henry drew from these passages and delivered to his church was simple: "The families of Christians should be little churches; wherever we have a house, God should have a church in it."[67]

Many have challenged Baxter's position on these passages and his view that they represent the family as a church. However, in a culture that is short on examples of worship in the home, they remain a great encouragement for us today. Even as a picture of the local church simply meeting in someone's home (as a house church), these

---

66. Ptacek, *Family Worship*, 27.
67. Henry, *Church in the House*, 23–25.

four passages remind us that prayers and praises can be enjoyed by Christian families in the home. With this possibility and opportunity, coupled with the worthiness of Christ, each individual Christian family has all of the reasons needed to cultivate prayers and praises together.

If Family Worship Includes Teaching, It Must Also Include Prayer

Baxter's tenth encouragement for family prayer and praise seems to recall his second proposition—namely, that family worship ought to include teaching the Word of God. Here he wrote, "If rulers must teach their families the Word of God, then they must pray with them."[68] Since he had already demonstrated the antecedent, he focused on proving the consequent.

His encouragement was fourfold. Baxter first noted the pairing of teaching and prayer in Acts 20:36. Second, he recognized that those who are teaching the Scriptures have a special need for the Lord's help in allowing them to understand the mind and Word of God so that His Word may be beneficial and profitable. One may seek this help through prayer.

The third reason why families should couple prayer and teaching in the home appeals to the reverence of worship. Baxter asserted that teaching the Scriptures is such a holy duty that prayer is required. Finally, Baxter mentioned Philippians 4:6 again and emphasized that if "in every thing by prayer" truly includes everything, then it will also include family teaching. He concluded with an appeal to the reader's own conscience: "I think that few men who are convinced of the duty of reading Scripture and solemnly instructing their families will question the duty of praying for God's blessing on it when they wet upon the work."[69]

Doolittle also drew a connection between family teaching and prayer. He began with the premise that the head of the home ought

---

68. Baxter, *Godly Home*, 84.
69. Baxter, *Godly Home*, 84.

to put the Scriptures in front of his family, instructing them with the Word of God. This responsibility to teach naturally brings a responsibility to prayer. Doolittle wrote, "The reason of this consequence, from family reading and instructions to family praying, is evident."[70] He then outlines six arguments for his position. These include the simple truths that since it is God's Word being taught, He must be sought in prayer; since the Word contains deep and mysterious doctrines, prayer for understanding is imperative; and since it is the Spirit of God who must pierce the heart with the Word, families must lift up prayers for the Lord to transform one another's hearts.[71]

In the nineteenth century, J. W. Alexander wrote on family worship. Like Baxter, he held biblical teaching and prayer together: "The hour of domestic prayer and praise is also the hour of Scriptural instruction."[72] Alexander further connected the responsibility of teaching the Word of God with the need to pray for this ability.

Families Learning How to Pray Must Also Pray Together

As with many of his points, Baxter's eleventh argument takes advantage of an if-then clause: "If rulers of families are bound to teach their families to pray, then they are bound to pray with them."[73] Baxter offered three Scriptures in support of the antecedent. He revisited Ephesians 6:4 and the charge for parents to bring their children up "in the nurture and admonition of the Lord." Baxter asserted that such discipline and instruction will include teaching children how to pray. Psalm 34:11 and Proverbs 22:6 are also referenced. Baxter concluded with these passages, writing, "They are bound to 'teach the fear of the Lord' and to 'train up a child in the way he should go,' and that is doubtless the way of prayer and praising God."[74]

---

70. Thomas Doolittle, "The Word of God and Family Prayer," in Pollard and Brown, *Theology of the Family*, 71.

71. Doolittle, "Word of God and Family Prayer," 71–73.

72. J. W. Alexander, "The Father and Family Worship," in Pollard and Brown, *Theology of the Family*, 84.

73. Baxter, *Godly Home*, 84.

74. Baxter, *Godly Home*, 85.

The rest of the argument, then, aims to strengthen the consequence. If heads of household are called to teach family members how to pray, then they are also called to pray with them. Baxter did not offer any additional Scriptures, but he did provide an illustration and an appeal to experience.

Baxter compared teaching prayer to teaching music, arguing that one would always find the teacher and the student actually playing music together and not just talking about music. The appeal to experience simply challenges the reader to consider the method in which they learned to pray and to recall whether they learned prayer without ever seeing it practiced before them. Baxter further argued that even if one has such an experience, that would be rare and should not be expected as ordinary for the rest. Baxter's final push, then, is that "they who must teach them to pray must pray with them."[75]

Family Meals Necessitate Family Prayers

Baxter's next support for family prayers and praises proves one of the most practical and, perhaps, accessible, as he contended for household prayer based on something every family can relate to sharing—meals. First Timothy 4:4–5 drives the appeal: "For every creature of God is good, and nothing to be refused, if it be received with thanksgiving: for it is sanctified by the word of God and prayer." The context includes receiving meals with thanksgiving, and it is in this context that Baxter draws application for families of his day. As Oliver Heywood wrote, "Take your family at mealtime to seek God."[76] Since families share meals together and meals are to include a time of prayer and thanksgiving, then family meals will include family prayers. Baxter noted, "They eat together; therefore they must give thanks together."[77] Ptacek picked up this same theme as he acknowledged that the call to

---

75. Baxter, *Godly Home*, 85.
76. Oliver Heywood, *A Family Altar Erected to the Honour of the Eternal God, or, a Solemn Essay to Promote the Worship of God in Private Houses Being Some Meditations on Genesis 35:2–3* (England: EEBO Editions ProQuest, 2011), 133.
77. Baxter, *Godly Home*, 86.

give thanks evokes an element of family worship, specifically while receiving meals together.[78]

The Joint Prayer of a Husband and Wife Is Required

In Baxter's encouragement of family prayers, the call for husbands to pray with their wives receives brief attention. The brevity, however, does not imply that it is less important than other aspects of family worship. Instead, Baxter seems to expect little opposition as he moves quickly through this point.

He wrote out 1 Peter 3:7 and discussed the sorts of prayers that may be hindered in the home when husbands and wives allow "ignorant and unkind conversation."[79] Private prayer may suffer in this context, but Baxter asserted that the passage primarily has in view the joint prayer between a husband and wife: "With what hearts can husband and wife join together as one soul in prayer to God when they abuse and exasperate each other and come hot from chidings and dissensions? This seems the true meaning of the text."[80] In Baxter's mind, the result and proper application for the reader is that "the joint prayer of husband and wife" is proved to be a duty.[81]

Like Baxter's writings, Richard Steele's sermon also engaged 1 Peter 3:7, which he quickly applied to family prayer. The relevant section of his sermon is even titled "Mutual Prayer." Steele taught that Peter's words imply that husbands and wives "should pray for and with one another…for there is no better preservative of real love and peace than praying together."[82]

Donald Whitney addressed the prayers of 1 Peter 3:7 and also understood this verse to speak of the joint prayer between a husband and a wife. He wrote, "Have you realized that the prayers here are those prayed together by husbands and wives?"[83] Whitney affirmed,

---

78. Ptacek, *Family Worship*, 31.
79. Baxter, *Godly Home*, 86.
80. Baxter, *Godly Home*, 86.
81. Baxter, *Godly Home*, 86.
82. Steele, "What Are the Duties?," 281.
83. Whitney, *Family Worship*, 26.

"The text speaks of mutual prayer. Peter assumes that Christian couples pray together. He expected Christian husbands to conduct family worship."[84]

Mutual prayer between a husband and wife can be one of the most accessible disciplines for those looking to practice family worship. As one starts the journey of implementing family worship, one would do well to begin by praying with their spouse. When a husband and wife pray together regularly, their hearts become unified and more and more inclined to also join together in praise and in the teaching of the Word of God.

Colossians 3:16–18 Presents a Case for Family Prayer

Baxter referenced Colossians 3:16–18 several times throughout his argument, and in his fourteenth point he leaned on this passage to claim a strong case for family prayer. Baxter offered a miniature three-point sermon on family prayer from this passage.

The first point considers that the call to enjoy praises and thanksgiving with one another comes in the context of Paul addressing families. Baxter reminded the reader that verses immediately following this passage will address wives, husbands, children, and parents. Therefore, one may assume that Colossians 3:16–18 should be lived out within the home. The second point speaks to those who may argue that the "one another" language of Colossians 3:16–18 is not intended for families. Here Baxter concedes, "If neighbors are bound to speak together in psalms, hymns, and spiritual songs, with grace in their hearts to the Lord, and to continue in prayer and thanksgiving, then families much more so."[85]

Baxter drew his sermon to a close with his third and final point. Colossians 3:17 reads, "And whatsoever ye do in word or deed, do all in the name of the Lord Jesus, giving thanks to God and the Father by him." Since families share many daily tasks together, in word and

---

84. Whitney, *Family Worship*, 26.
85. Baxter, *Godly Home*, 87.

also in deed, they are called to share this daily business while giving thanks to the Lord together.

Joel Beeke also applied Colossians 3:16–18 to the duty of families to worship by singing praises to God. He asserted that families are to praise God with grace in their hearts. He also contended that singing the psalms and hymns proves especially powerful, for this sort of worship finds the family singing God's Word together. In considering this text, Beeke wrote, "We must implement family worship in the home…. The Lord Jesus is worthy of it, God's Word commands it, and conscience affirms it as our duty."[86] Beeke therefore not only supported Baxter's application of Colossians 3:16 but also affirmed his overall argument that family worship is one's duty before the Lord.

If Households Must Serve the Lord, They Must Also Pray and Praise

The if-then clause of this argument assumes the former statement, that households must serve the Lord, while aiming to prove the latter statement, that families must then also pray to the Lord and praise Him. Joshua serves as Baxter's example. Joshua 24:15 finds Joshua declaring, "But as for me and my house, we will serve the LORD." Baxter observed, "Prayer and praise are so necessary parts of God's service that no family or person can be said in general to be devoted to serve God that are not devoted to them."[87] Donald Whitney also affirms Joshua 24:15 as a call to family worship: "Regular family worship of some sort would have been a part of carrying out Joshua's resolve."[88]

Thomas Doolittle's sermon on Joshua 24:15 asked whether it is the duty of families to pray together. He understood *house* in this passage to include one's family and interpreted "serving the Lord" to include prayer as one of the manners in which a household may serve the Lord together. He claimed, "Calling upon God is such an

---

86. Beeke, *Family Worship*, 14.
87. Baxter, *Godly Home*, 87.
88. Whitney, *Family Worship*, 20.

eminent part of worship, and such a principal way of serving the Lord, that it is frequently put for the whole worship of God."[89]

Doolittle stated that the Holy Spirit led Joshua to make this bold declaration. The foundation for this position is found in verse 2 as Joshua makes it clear that the first thirteen verses are directly from the Lord. Doolittle's sermon continued by claiming that it was in the name of God that Joshua exhorted the rest of the families to also serve the Lord in their homes. Doolittle taught that in Joshua's resolution, he, "like a prudent governor, draweth them on to imitate him."[90] It seems that Baxter picked up this same task in encouraging his church to imitate Joshua's example by practicing family prayer and praise.

As George Hamond applied Joshua 24:15 to family worship, he anticipated objections from those who may conclude that worship or prayers are not in view as Joshua promises that his family would serve the Lord. Some might interpret this as a broad or perhaps even ambiguous statement that includes more than just these elements. Hamond aimed to silence such objections. He concluded that this passage clearly points to family worship, "unless it could be shown that serving the Lord either excludes or is inconsistent with worshipping him."[91] Assuming that such exclusions or inconsistencies do not exist, he repeated his application of Joshua 24:15, that families who serve the Lord will enjoy worshiping, praying, and praising together.

Fearing God Includes Prayer

If you were to describe a family that prays together, would you assume that they fear God? To put it another way, if you were to describe a family that fears God, what would you assume about their prayer life? Baxter's next encouragement asserts that those who fear God will also pray together.

Just as Cornelius "feared God with all his house" (Acts 10:2), families today are to come together in the fear of God. Baxter connects

---

89. Doolittle, "How May the Duty?," 200.
90. Doolittle, "How May the Duty?," 202.
91. Hamond, *Case for Family Worship*, 59.

this fear with prayer, which he also sees in Acts 10. Cornelius prayed in his home (Acts 10:30) and gathered his relatives and close friends together to hear from the Lord (Acts 10:24). These aspects of the life of Cornelius led Baxter to conclude, "When he is said to fear God with all his house, it is also meant that he worshipped God with his house; and that he used to do it together with them is implied in his gathering together his kindred."[92]

Hamond's works agree with Baxter's interpretation of Acts 10 and noted Cornelius as a prime example of one who led in family worship. As Hamond boldly attested, "This is so plain and pregnant a proof that Cornelius maintained family worship that I cannot conceive what paraphrase can be made use of to illustrate it but the multiplying of words will rather darken it."[93] He clearly believed that for Cornelius to fear God with his household would indeed include worshiping God with his family.

Managing One's Household Includes Leading in Family Prayer

Baxter also proposed that family worship will include the teaching of God's Word. He defended that position by referencing the requirement in 1 Timothy 3 that overseers and deacons would manage their households before setting out to manage the church. Included in this proposition was the conclusion that family worship will include leading in prayer and praises: "Now, to rule the church is to teach and guide it as their mouth in prayer and praises unto God as well as to oversee their lives. Therefore, it is such a ruling of their houses that is a prerequisite to prove them fit."[94]

If caring for God's church includes guiding other believers in prayer to and praise of God, then caring for one's household will involve the same. Baxter assumed the former and proposed the latter. He interpreted the text to mean that "it is the duty of masters of

---

92. Baxter, *Godly Home*, 88.
93. Hamond, *Case for Family Worship*, 77.
94. Baxter, *Godly Home*, 88.

families to rule well, instructing their families in the right worshipping of God…as ministers must rule the church."[95]

As Jay Adams discussed the 1 Timothy command to manage one's household, he too engaged the subject of family prayer. To manage one's household well, one must be zealous in his spiritual leadership. Adams argued that husbands and fathers should be "most zealous to see that leadership was exercised in family worship…in family prayer."[96]

Andreas Köstenberger also connected the responsibility of spiritual headship of the home with that of family prayer, although he did not specifically reference 1 Timothy 3. In writing on family worship, he championed the kind of spiritual leadership of fathers that focuses on discipleship, including joint prayer.[97]

Some Prayer Requests Are Best Suited for Joint Family Prayer

Baxter assumed three sorts of prayers in this argument: private or individual prayer, family prayer, and corporate prayer with the entire church body. He suggested that families have shared needs that go beyond private or individual prayer yet do not need to be made as public as corporate prayer requests. These sorts of prayer needs, then, are best suited for family prayer. Baxter wrote, "Families have family necessities that are larger than can be confined to a closet and yet more private than to be brought into the assemblies of the church."[98]

The necessities in mind are disagreements or needs that the entire family shares. These concern the whole family and therefore must be prayed for in joint prayer. However, they are of a private nature so that they do not need to be shared with the entire church body. Furthermore, if every family in the church reserved these sort of prayer requests for the church assembly, there would be so many

---

95. Baxter, *Godly Home*, 89.
96. Jay E. Adams, *Christian Living in the Home* (Phillipsburg, N.J.: P&R Publishing, 1972), 93.
97. Köstenberger, *God, Marriage, and Family*, 171.
98. Baxter, *Godly Home*, 89.

prayer requests that the minister would be overwhelmed and the public worship would have time for little else.

Aside from these considerations, Baxter closed his argument with four additional points of motivation. First, he suggested that as family members may often sin together, they should confess in prayer together while sharing in the lamentation over such sin. Second, since families receive mercies and blessings from God together, praising Him together is best suited for family prayer rather than corporate prayer. Third, as families often work together, their prayers seeking the Lord's help with this work is best suited for the home. Finally, when families confess in front of one another, there is accountability and an increased encouragement to flee from sin.

God Never Reversed His Order for Family Prayer or Worship

As Baxter concluded his encouragement for family worship to include prayer and praises, he challenged any objector to demonstrate from Scripture when God suspended or discontinued the call for family prayer and worship. Baxter highlighted the examples of Cain and Abel, Noah, Abraham, and Jacob, who offered their own sacrifices. His point was that the head of a household was meant to serve as a priest to his own family.

Baxter then anticipated the objection that this somehow changed once the office of the priest was instituted. He argued that this did not discontinue family worship, noting that the sacraments of circumcision and the Passover continued in the home even after the office of the priest was instituted. He resolved that there is not "a word of Scripture that speaks of God reversing his command or order for family prayer or other family worship. Therefore, it is still obligatory."[99]

Köstenberger supported this position. Just as Scripture commands families to teach the Word of God within the home, families today share this same responsibility. Moreover, it remains God's will for families today. No command has been given to reverse what is seen in Scripture. Köstenberger wrote, "God's express will for his

---

99. Baxter, *Godly Home*, 91.

people Israel is still his will for God's people in the church today. Christian parents have the mandate and serious obligation to instill their religious heritage in their children."[100]

This heritage is a legacy of faith that parents pass on to the next generation. Through family worship—including teaching the Word of God, praying together, and singing praises with one another— heads of households have the great opportunity and privilege of passing on the gospel to their children and their children's children. Instead of focusing solely on a worldly inheritance or heirlooms that may be handed down, families today are called to embrace worshiping together so that faith in Jesus may endure as their lasting heritage.

Objections Answered

Baxter concluded his encouragement for family worship by answering four objections. The first challenge to his belief that family worship is God's will claims that there is only a handful of Scriptures that present this duty. Baxter answered by first reminding the hypothetical objector that he had demonstrated clearly that family worship is required in the Scriptures. His propositions and supporting arguments offer more than fifty Scriptures as support. Furthermore, Baxter restated some of the general principles for prayer and praise in the Scriptures and their natural application to the home.

Beeke also answered this objection in a like manner. He conceded that the Bible does not contain an explicit command for family worship. However, after examining many of the same Scriptures supporting Baxter's argument, he concluded that it is "clear that God would have families worship him daily."[101]

The second objection reads, "Christ himself did not often pray with his family, as appears by the disciples asking him to teach them to pray and by the silence of the Scripture on this point. Therefore, it is not our duty."[102] Baxter exposed the argument of silence as weak,

---

100. Köstenberger, *God, Marriage, and Family*, 102.
101. Beeke, *Family Worship*, 35.
102. Baxter, *Godly Home*, 92.

pointing out that Jesus did many things that were not written. For the remainder of his response, Baxter focused on the relationship between Jesus and His disciples, for in Matthew 12:46–50, Jesus identified His disciples as family. Baxter noted passages such as Luke 22:17–18, Mark 14:22–26, and Matthew 26:27–30 to illustrate that Jesus did frequently pray with His disciples and sing hymns to the Lord with them. Baxter also contended that many needs which families have for household worship were not shared by Jesus. An example of this would be a family's need to confess sins together in prayer.

For the third objection, Baxter expected that some might suggest prayers offered to the Lord by wicked families would displease God and therefore not be required as a duty. Baxter refused to concede this concern. Instead, he continued to advance his arguments for family worship. He began by stating that this objection does not at all speak to godly families and their responsibility to worship together. Neither would this objection apply to godly fathers leading ungodly family members in worship and prayer, for in this the Lord is honored by the faithfulness of the head of the household. Moreover, Jesus prayed while the ungodly Judas was present.[103]

Concerning the prayers of the wicked, Baxter contended that these prayers are not wicked or displeasing to the Lord if the prayers are genuine prayers of repentance. In support of this position, Baxter directed the reader to consider Acts 8:22, in which Peter told the sinful Simon Magus to repent and pray to the Lord. Baxter concluded his third response as he wrote, "So let the wicked pray, and his prayer will not be abominable."[104]

The fourth and final objection states, "Many masters of families cannot pray in their families without a book, and that is unlawful."[105] This objection invites Baxter's shortest reply. He offered two possible solutions. First, the head of the home is to seek growth in order to

---

103. Baxter, *Godly Home*, 93.
104. Baxter, *Godly Home*, 93.
105. Baxter, *Godly Home*, 94.

overcome his shortcomings.[106] Second, as he grows, he is permitted to use a prayer book in the time of family worship, for this is preferable to not praying at all.

Beeke, acknowledging those who do not feel capable of leading family worship, offered a similar response and made a few suggestions. He first recommended several books as helpful resources meant to strengthen one in his leadership of the home. Beeke also proposed that one request their pastor to visit their home and model family worship for them, teaching how to lead. Heads of homes are also encouraged simply to begin implementing family worship, trusting that they will grow stronger in their leadership with practice. Finally, he upheld the petitioning of the Holy Spirit and dependence on Him as the most important aspects of learning how to lead in family worship.[107]

---

106. Donald Miller's 1935 dissertation portrayed Baxter as a pastor who would visit homes where the spiritual leadership was weak, in order to model worship for the family. He would read the Word of God and pray with the family for the purpose of training them in worship. This "object lesson" afforded the heads of households an opportunity to observe the manner in which they were to lead. Donald G. Miller, "A Critical Appraisal of Richard Baxter's Views of the Church and Their Applicability to Contemporary Church Problems," (PhD diss., New York University, 1935), 151.

107. Beeke, *Family Worship*, 37–38.

CHAPTER SIX

Baxter's Family-Equipping Ministry at Kidderminster

Baxter was not content simply to teach about family worship or put forth a theological foundation. He built on this and sought to offer a practical theology so that families actually practiced worshiping together and could truly enjoy the transforming power of Christ in their homes.

Baxter's conviction that family worship is God's will led him to equip families through preaching, home visits, catechesis, church discipline, and counseling. The biblical pattern of equipping families with the Word of God is seen in passages such as Deuteronomy 6:4–9, Psalm 78:1–8, Joshua 24:14–15, Ephesians 6:4, and 2 Timothy 1:5.

Jay Strother applied several of these texts to arrive at an understanding of equipping families. He examined Deuteronomy 6:7 and the Hebrew phrase *shanan*, meaning "to chisel in stone." Strother concluded that to impress the Word of God on the next generation, one must chisel it into their lives. "A key objective for the entire church is to equip and support parents in making their homes ministry centers for the spiritual growth of their children."[1]

For Baxter, preaching, home visits, catechesis, church discipline, and counseling served as primary ways to chisel God's Word into the hearts of families. His entire pastoral ministry focused on these aspects of equipping his community to grow in Christ and lead

---

1. Jay Strother, "Family-Equipping Ministry: Church and Home as Cochampions," in *Perspectives on Family Ministry: 3 Views*, ed. Timothy Paul Jones (Nashville, Tenn.: B&H Academic, 2009), 151.

their families to do the same. J. I. Packer concluded, "In Baxter's Kidderminster ministry appears the full flowering of the Puritan pastoral ideal."[2]

While Baxter's years in Kidderminster found him unmarried, he adopted a view that the church families were his family. In fact, he believed his singleness and lack of any children of his own created more opportunities for his family ministry in the church: "I found that my single life afforded me much advantage; for I could easily take my people for my children, and think all that I had too little for them, in that I had no children of my own to tempt me to another way of using it. And being discharged from the most of family cares I had the greater vacancy and liberty for the labors of my calling."[3]

The success of this family ministry is seen in the reformation that took place in Kidderminster during Baxter's time as pastor. The town was transformed as just about every family that had once neglected family worship began to practice it faithfully. J. Lewis Wilson reflected on this fruit and considered it one of the strongest examples of Puritan family ministry: "The transformation of Kidderminster under Baxter and his assistants is another permanent example to bear witness to Puritan achievement in family religion."[4]

---

2. Packer, *Redemption and Restoration of Man*, 52.

3. Baxter, *Autobiography of Richard Baxter*, 80–81. Baxter did later marry Margaret Charlton in 1662, two years after he concluded his ministry in Kidderminster. Marcus L. Loane's book *Makers of Puritan History* offers an abridged version of Baxter's biography. Loane wrote on Baxter's personal family worship practices with his wife, Margaret. The married couple would begin and end each day with a psalm of praise. See Loane, *Makers of Puritan History*, 223. Robert McCan's dissertation offered an expanded description: "Richard and Margaret sang a psalm of praise each night just before bed, and again each morning when they awoke, until irate neighbors made them stop." Robert L. McCan, "The Conception of the Church in Richard Baxter and John Bunyan: A Comparison and Contrast," (PhD diss., University of Edinburgh, 1955), 36.

4. J. Lewis Wilson, "Catechisms and the Puritans," in *Puritan Papers, Volume Four: 1965–1967*, ed. J. I. Packer (Phillipsburg, N.J.: P&R Publishing, 2004), 148.

Preaching

The Puritan movement as a whole held a high view of biblical preaching, leading some to call it "the golden age of preaching."[5] The Puritan ethos valued preaching as that which the Lord would use to build His church. Preaching therefore remained the minister's chief task. Leland Ryken wrote, "It was through the pulpit that Puritanism made its mark on the English nation."[6] Therefore, it was the pulpit, instead of an altar, that appeared in the center of Puritan churches.[7]

The substance of Puritan preaching was simply "declaring God's Word to men."[8] Packer pointed to Baxter's preaching as one of the greatest aspects of his fruitful ministry in Kidderminster: "The key element in his success, humanly speaking, was undoubtedly the clarity, force, and skill with which he communicated the gospel itself."[9] Baxter's conviction that family worship is God's will complemented his view of preaching, which considered the minister a partner in the family worship ministry. Heads of household were called to teach and catechize within the home, yet Baxter recognized that ministers were often more equipped and prepared to teach the fullness of Scripture, including more difficult passages. Therefore, family worship included an encouragement to adhere to the preaching of God's Word and a submission to the pastoral leaders within the church. Baxter wrote, "Family teaching must stand in subordination to ministerial teaching.... Family teaching must give place to ministerial teaching and never be set against it.... Therefore, when any hard text or controversies fall in, the head should consult with the pastor for their exposition."[10]

Baxter preached once every Lord's Day and once every Thursday evening. A weekly pastor's forum was also implemented to allow

---

5. Joel R. Beeke, *Reformed Preaching: Proclaiming God's Word from the Heart of the Preacher to the Heart of His People* (Wheaton, Ill.: Crossway, 2018), 142.

6. Ryken, *Worldly Saints*, 91.

7. Beeke, *Reformed Preaching*, 145.

8. Beeke, *Reformed Preaching*, 144.

9. Packer, *Puritan Portraits*, 170.

10. Baxter, *Godly Home*, 71–72.

space for prayer and discussion.[11] Baxter described some of the unique aspects of his preaching ministry and the ways in which he applied them to ministry in the home: "Every Thursday evening my neighbors that were most desirous and had opportunity met at my house, and there one of them repeated the sermon, and afterwards they proposed what doubts any of them had about the sermon, or any other case of conscience, and I resolved their doubts; and last of all I caused sometimes one and sometimes another of them to pray; and sometimes I prayed with them myself."[12]

The younger generation would also meet together once a week on Saturday nights to review Baxter's sermons. They would spend three hours in prayer together, then discuss the sermon from the previous Sunday. Finally, this group would prepare themselves for the following day of worship with the church.[13]

Throughout Baxter's rigorous preaching schedule that included the intentional post-sermon discussions and home visits, his health continued to plague him with weakness. However, this seemed to pale in comparison to his spiritual vigor, and it also motivated an urgency in his preaching. Baxter reflected on this impact: "Another advantage was that at first I was in the vigor of my spirits and had naturally a familiar moving voice (which is a great matter with the common hearers); and doing all in bodily weakness, as a dying man, my soul was the more easily brought to seriousness, and to preach as a dying man to dying men."[14]

Baxter gave all the glory for his fruitful preaching ministry to the Lord. He shared this praise in his autobiography, writing, "I bless God who gave me…such liberty and advantage to preach his Gospel with success."[15] His dependence on the Lord for his preaching is evident in his view of the relationship between preaching and prayer. He wrote, "Our whole work must be carried on under a deep sense of our own

---

11. Baxter, *Reformed Pastor*, 13.
12. Baxter, *Autobiography of Richard Baxter*, 77.
13. Baxter, *Autobiography of Richard Baxter*, 77.
14. Baxter, *Autobiography of Richard Baxter*, 79.
15. Baxter, *Autobiography of Richard Baxter*, 80.

insufficiency, and of our entire dependence on Christ.... Prayer must carry on our work as well as preaching: he preacheth not heartily to his people, that prayeth not earnestly for them."[16] Baxter's fellowship and relationship with the Lord directly impacted and influenced his preaching. As Leith Samuel noted, "It was evident that he preached from love of the Savior, not just from love of preaching."[17]

One of the most notable aspects of Baxter's preaching is seen in his desire to preach to himself before preaching to his church. Beeke viewed this as Baxter's desire to "pursue holiness in his own life" as he preached holiness to others.[18] Baxter allowed God's Word and every sermon to reach his heart so that his preaching would be an overflow of what God had done in him. Paul Cook summarized this principle with four of Baxter's own convictions: "Baxter insists that a minister must (1) see that the work of saving grace is thoroughly wrought in his own soul; (2) take care to keep his Christian graces in vigilant and lively exercise, preaching first to himself all that he intends to preach to others, and watching constantly over his heart; (3) take heed lest his example contradict his doctrine; (4) take heed that he is not lacking the qualifications needed for his work."[19]

Edward Donnelly identified chief elements of Baxter's sermons, such as a repeated, logical structure: "First the opening of the text, then the removal of difficulties, followed by the uses and the appeal."[20] These sermons aimed to explain foundational truths with helpful application.

Plain preaching proved to be a hallmark of Puritan preaching. This approach found even the most educated preacher making their

---

16. Baxter, *Reformed Pastor*, 122.

17. Leith Samuel, "Richard Baxter and 'The Saints' Everlasting Rest,'" in *The Westminster Conference 1991: Advancing in Adversity* (London: Westminster Conference, 1991), 108.

18. Beeke, *Reformed Preaching*, 156.

19. Paul Cook, "The Life and Work of a Minister According to the Puritans," in *Puritan Papers, Volume One: 1956–1959*, ed. J. I. Packer (Phillipsburg, N.J.: P&R Publishing, 2000), 180.

20. Edward Connelly, introduction to *Dying Thoughts*, by Baxter, viii.

sermon simple so that the congregation could understand the Word of God. Beeke described this aspect of Puritan preaching: "Plainness referred to a simple and clear communication from the Bible to the mind, then into the heart, and then outward to direct the conduct."[21] Baxter clearly advocated for this approach. In his catechism for families, he wrote on the manner in which pastors should preach. Along with holy reverence, ministers were called to preach with great plainness and fervency.[22]

Packer also noted this plain style. He attributed Baxter's approach to other preachers who influenced his homiletic voice, such as Perkins, Sibbes, and Hooker, who employed this simplistic, plain preaching consisting of "short, terse sentences and vivid imagery, drawn from the Bible and everyday life."[23]

The simplicity of Baxter's sermons is seen in one of his sermons on 2 Corinthians 2:7. He began by opening the text: "Forgive and comfort him, lest perhaps such a one should be swallowed up with overmuch sorrow."[24] Baxter acknowledged some of the complexities of the passage and some of the debates surrounding the identity of the individual referenced in this verse. He had clearly studied these complexities and debates. Baxter was familiar with it all and perhaps even had his own conclusion. He even referenced some of these briefly in his introduction, recognizing Chrysostom's tradition that the one referenced was a doctor and Hamond's view that he was a bishop. However, Baxter avoided focusing on such speculation and instead ran straight to his main point, preaching the simple truth that there is a call to forgive and comfort, and a danger if this is neglected. Plain explanation and clear application were woven throughout the rest of the sermon.

Along with the aforementioned goals, Donnelly also recognized Baxter's passion for evangelism in his preaching. Constantly

---

21. Beeke, *Reformed Preaching*, 152–53.

22. Baxter, *Puritan Catechism for Families*, 317.

23. Packer, *Redemption and Restoration of Man*, 164.

24. Richard Baxter, "The Cure of Melancholy and Overmuch Sorrow," in *Puritan Sermons, 1659–1689*, 3:253.

driven by the conviction that all who heard his sermons would one day stand before Jesus Christ, Baxter preached with emotion, with eternity in mind, and with "words of piercing appeal springing from truth."[25] Baxter's sermons carried a clear invitation to receive Christ.

Home Visits and Catechesis Ministry

While Baxter's preaching ministry remained a focus throughout his time in Kidderminster, he recognized the unique value of both home visits and a family catechesis ministry, a value not necessarily achieved in preaching alone. Baxter observed, "I have found by experience, that some ignorant persons, who have been so long unprofitable hearers, have got more knowledge and remorse of conscience in half an hour's close discourse, than they did from ten years' public preaching."[26]

In fact, Baxter asserted that "personal catechizing and counseling, over and above preaching, is every minister's duty."[27] To this end, Baxter, along with his assistant, aimed to catechize every family in the church every year. They accomplished this by maintaining a demanding schedule of home visits. Baxter and his assistant invested two days, Monday and Tuesday, in privately catechizing fifteen to sixteen families every week of the year.[28] They would labor from early morning until the evening in this family ministry. Beeke described these visits, writing, "Those visits involved patiently teaching, gently examining, and carefully leading family and church members to Christ through the Scriptures."[29]

Any proper evaluation of Baxter's view of family worship will deal with his understanding of catechesis. He asserted that "personal catechizing and counseling, over and above preaching, is every minister's duty."[30] Baxter was not alone in his heart for a family catechesis

25. Donnelly, introduction to *Dying Thoughts*, by Baxter, xi.
26. Baxter, *Reformed Pastor*, 196.
27. Baxter, *Reformed Pastor*, 18.
28. Baxter, *Autobiography of Richard Baxter*, 77–78.
29. Beeke, *Puritan Evangelism*, 43.
30. Baxter, *Reformed Pastor*, 18.

ministry, as Beeke demonstrates: "The Puritans were catechists. They believed that pulpit messages should be reinforced by personalized ministry through catechesis—the instruction in the doctrines of Scripture using catechisms."[31] English Puritans of the seventeenth century viewed catechizing as a way to "open the door to the life of faith by laying faith's cognitive foundations."[32] As C. Jeffrey Robinson noted, the seventeenth-century Puritans ushered in a "golden age of catechisms and devotional works designed to be used in the teaching of children and in family worship."[33]

Baxter's convictions about family worship influenced his understanding of the catechesis ministry. He believed every family should receive a catechism to use in their home. "Baxter laid the responsibility for this instruction on parents."[34] The pastor would first model how to teach the catechisms, then the head of every family would teach the catechisms to their household every Sabbath evening. This was coupled with prayer and Scripture reading, along with other useful books that would edify and encourage the family.[35] Packer observed the unique approach Baxter took to the typical catechesis ministry: "To upgrade the practice of personal catechizing from a preliminary discipline for children to a permanent ingredient in evangelism and pastoral care for all ages was Baxter's main contribution to the development of Puritan ideals for the ministry."[36]

Given the central nature of catechesis in Baxter's ministry and the likelihood that this term is less familiar today, a definition seems useful. The term *catechesis* comes from the Greek verb *katche*. This is one of the words used in the New Testament for "teaching." Packer and Parrett defined this verb to mean "to share a communication that

---

31. Beeke, *Puritan Evangelism*, 63.
32. Packer, *Puritan Portraits*, 16.
33. Robinson, "Home Is an Earthly Kingdom," 124.
34. Wilson, "Catechisms and the Puritans," 146.
35. Baxter, *Reformed Pastor*, 100–101.
36. Packer, *Quest for Godliness*, 305.

one receives" and "to teach, instruct."[37] They wrote, "Catechesis is the church's ministry of grounding and growing God's people in the Gospel and its implications for doctrine, devotion, duty, and delight."[38]

Puritan catechisms were meant to convey "the sum of saving knowledge."[39] Baxter also took advantage of catechisms during his home visits in order to discern the impact of his preaching in the lives of his church families. With a heart that all would respond to Jesus, he longed to discover whether church members understood his sermons and were applying the Word of God to their lives. This required personal observation. As Donnelly noted, "His home visitation was a means of expanding and further applying what had been said in the pulpit. He found indeed that people would not take his preaching seriously unless it was enforced by close personal dealing."[40]

In his *Christian Directory*, Baxter addressed the use of catechisms as he presented a proper teaching for children. He advocated for a shorter catechism when the teaching begins before moving to a larger catechism as the child matures. The shorter and larger Westminster catechisms were specifically referenced.[41] Both of these catechisms consist of theological foundations, including a focus on the redemptive work of God, teachings on the Decalogue, sacraments, and the Lord's Prayer.[42] These are the very teachings that fifty-year-old Baxter described as his "daily bread and drink."[43]

Baxter wrote two catechisms in his *Poor Man's Family Book* and added a third with *A Puritan Catechism for Families*. One of the primary uses of these catechisms would be for the heads of families who would "endeavor to raise their children…to a good degree of

37. J. I. Packer and Gary A. Parrett, *Grounded in the Gospel: Building Believers the Old-Fashioned Way* (Grand Rapids: Baker, 2010), 27.

38. Packer and Parrett, *Grounded in the Gospel*, 29.

39. Packer, *Redemption and Restoration of Man*, 43.

40. Donnelly, introduction to *Dying Thoughts*, by Baxter, xvi.

41. Baxter, *Godly Home*, 218.

42. Packer and Parrett, *Grounded in the Gospel*, 86.

43. Packer, *Evangelical Influences*, 28.

knowledge."[44] His own catechism supports the argument that the seventeenth-century Puritans viewed the ministry of catechesis as a means of equipping families with God's Word. Heads of households were meant to teach one chapter at a time "on the Lord's days, or at nights, when they have leisure."[45]

While some of Baxter's early years in ministry found him engaging controversies, his later years carried the reflection that these were no longer of great value. Instead, he intentionally shifted his focus to more simple and basic matters. At fifty years old, he wrote, "It is the fundamental doctrines of the catechism which I highliest value and daily think of, and find most useful to myself and others."[46]

Other Puritans who developed their own catechisms include John Bunyan and Benjamin Keach. *Bunyan's Catechism* was first published in 1675.[47] Bunyan aimed to remind the church of the first things while also providing truth that may lead to the awakening and salvation of the unconverted. He considered the ministry of catechesis to be a token of his love for the church. *Keach's Catechism* of 1677 also demonstrates the emphasis on catechesis during this time period. Keach viewed his catechism as a "short account of Christian principles, for the instruction of our families."[48]

Thomas Lye also preached on the necessity and value of catechizing children in the home. He not only upheld this discipleship method as a way to protect children from temptation while equipping them with the truth but also believed that catechisms were an effective form of memorization. He taught, "This manner of teaching by way of catechizing, (namely, by propounding the question, and putting the child to answer it, as the echo doth the voice), is a most ready way to make any instruction to take."[49]

---

44. Baxter, *Puritan Catechism for Families*, viii.

45. Baxter, *Puritan Catechism for Families*, ix.

46. As quoted in Packer, *Evangelical Influences*, 28.

47. John Bunyan, *Bunyan's Catechism* (Choteau, Mont.: Old Paths Gospel Press, 2008).

48. Benjamin Keach, *Keach's Catechism* (Edinburgh: CrossReach Publications, 2017), 4.

49. Lye, "By What Scriptural Rules?," 105.

J. Lewis Wilson published an article titled "Catechisms and the Puritans" in which he explored "the basic convictions which guided Puritan pastors (like Baxter) in their use of catechism."[50] Wilson noted that Baxter defended his use of catechism with a purpose of teaching the greatest points of Scripture that are necessary for salvation. Although Baxter catechized those in his church, Wilson wrote that he "laid the responsibility of this instruction on parents."[51] This method of equipping families with God's Word and biblical doctrines remained central for many Puritan pastors. However, Wilson argued, "the most significant and possibly the most effective of all Puritan attempts in catechizing took place immediately before the Restoration in the achievement of Richard Baxter and his associates at Kidderminster and in the wider Worcestershire Association."[52] Wilson concluded, "It is in Baxter's work that Puritan ideals reach in great measure, their fulfillment and their crown."[53]

Baxter's approach to equipping families through catechisms influenced many pastors in the coming generations, continuing well past his tenure in Kidderminster. About two hundred years later, Charles Spurgeon still advocated for the inclusion of catechisms in family ministry. Puritans like Baxter heavily influenced Spurgeon's catechesis ministry.[54] Spurgeon leaned on Baxter's example and considered him "the most forceful of writers."[55] The title of Spurgeon's catechism, *A Puritan Catechism*, demonstrates this influence. J. I. Packer even referred to Spurgeon as a "latter day Puritan."[56] Arthur Bennett also recognized Spurgeon's relation to the Puritans, referring to him as "the last of the great Puritans."[57]

---

50. Wilson, "Catechisms and the Puritans," 140.

51. Wilson, "Catechisms and the Puritans," 146.

52. Wilson, "Catechisms and the Puritans," 153.

53. Wilson, "Catechisms and the Puritans," 153.

54. Charles H. Spurgeon, *A Puritan Catechism with Proofs* (Lexington, Ky.: Legacy Publications, 2011).

55. As quoted in J. I. Packer, introduction to *Reformed Pastor*, by Baxter,16.

56. Packer, *Quest for Godliness*, 69.

57. Arthur Bennett, ed., *The Valley of Vision: A Collection of Puritan Prayers and Devotions* (Carlisle, Pa.: Banner of Truth, 2017), 1.

Charles Spurgeon was only nineteen years old when God called him to serve as the pastor of New Park Street Chapel in London, England. He was single and had no children of his own, and he was pastoring a church filled with families. Spurgeon understood his call to invest in families, even at nineteen, and by the time he was twenty-one years old he published his own catechism for the families of his church.

Spurgeon primarily borrowed from the Westminster Shorter Catechism and the London Baptist Catechism. The Westminster Shorter Catechism was published in 1648 for the churches of Scotland, England, and Ireland. The shorter version came a year after the Larger Catechism, which proved even longer than the Westminster Confession of Faith.[58] The London Baptist Confession of Faith was published in 1689.[59] Four years later, in 1693, the Baptist Catechism was published with the purpose of teaching the London Baptist Confession. This catechism is attributed to Benjamin Keach (who had also served as pastor of New Park Street Chapel) and William Collins.[60]

Spurgeon's conviction was that families would benefit from using a good catechism in their homes. Following Baxter's example, Spurgeon led families to teach and enjoy God's Word together. He wrote, "The first and most natural responsibility is for Christian parents to train up their own children in the nurture and admonition of the Lord."[61]

Counseling

Packer discussed the various pastoral duties present in the Puritan ministries and specifically addressed Baxter's. Packer wrote,

---

58. Rogers, *Presbyterian Creeds*, 156.

59. Peter Masters, ed., *The Baptist Confession of Faith 1689: The Second London Confession with Scripture Proofs from the Edition of C. H. Spurgeon, 1855* (London: Wakeman Trust, 2008), 5.

60. William L. Lumpkin, *Baptist Confessions of Faith* (Valley Forge, Pa.: Judson Press, 1969), 240.

61. Charles H. Spurgeon, *Come Ye Children: Obtaining Our Lord's Heart for Loving and Teaching Children* (Abbotsford, Wis.: Aneko Press, 2017), 57.

"Puritanism's spearhead activity was pastoral evangelism and nurture through preaching, catechizing, and counseling (which Puritan pastors called 'casuistry,' the resolving of 'cases of conscience')."[62] This sort of counseling became a bedrock in Baxter's family ministry.

Counseling had become a chief aspect of Puritan pastoral ministry by the time Baxter began preaching. Mark Deckard's recent work on the Puritans' example of biblical counseling presents a robust ministry still applicable today. Deckard examined seven Puritan leaders and their writings on counseling issues, including addiction, anxiety, depression, and grief. He concluded, "In each area these Puritan authors have direct contributions to make towards our ministry with people today."[63]

William Perkins was one of the Puritan pioneers in counseling. He viewed the pastor as a spiritual physician pointing others to Christ, the healer.[64] The connection between physician and counselor was one to which Baxter could relate. Kidderminster lacked a physician. Baxter therefore found himself taking on as many as twenty patients a day. Although he enjoyed more success than expected, the medical ministry distracted him from his other responsibilities and studies. After filling this role for a few years, Baxter convinced a trained physician to come and live in Kidderminster, which freed him to once again focus wholeheartedly on the ministry of the church.[65]

His time as a physician afforded Baxter a lasting illustration of soul care and the similarities between a doctor and a pastor. He wrote, "A minister is not to be merely a public preacher, but to be known as a counsellor for their souls, as the physician is for their bodies."[66]

Baxter's counseling ministry proved a dominant aspect of his family ministry in Kidderminster. He believed that "one word of seasonable, prudent advice, given by a minister to persons in necessity,

---

62. Packer, *Evangelical Influences*, 226–27.

63. Deckard, *Helpful Truth in Past Places*, 208.

64. Nathaniel Harrington Mair, "Christian Sanctification and Individual Pastoral Care in Richard Baxter," (PhD diss., Union Theological Seminary, 1967), 51.

65. Baxter, *Autobiography of Richard Baxter*, 78.

66. Baxter, *Reformed Pastor*, 96.

may be of more use than many sermons."[67] Pastoral counseling seemed to Baxter a forgotten aspect of ministry, so he undertook it as his duty to invite church members to come to the pastor for counsel. He wrote, "It belongeth to us to acquaint them with it (counseling), and publicly to press them to come to us for advice about the great concerns of their souls."[68] He believed that such encouragement would lead church members to frequently knock on the doors of the pastor and other ministers for the purpose of expressing their concerns while seeking counsel.[69]

This opportunity is specifically observed in Baxter's counseling of those who are depressed. He encouraged family members to bring the one struggling with depression to their pastor: "Ensure that they are under the care of a prudent and capable Christian pastor, both for confidential counsel and for public preaching.... Make sure this minister is skillful in dealing with depressed parishioners.... Direct depressed persons to a pastor whom they already admire and respect and will listen to."[70] Baxter also viewed family worship as necessary in one's ministry to a family member battling depression. He called family members to encourage the one who is depressed with the "great truths of the gospel that are likeliest to bring them comfort."[71]

As with the other aspects of his Kidderminster ministry, Baxter's counseling was also informed by his conviction that family worship is God's will. He understood that any soul care would be undone in the church by worldly families. Conversely, the ministry would be encouraged by families who pray and worship together. Therefore, ministers aiming to counsel must "have a special eye upon

---

67. Baxter, *Reformed Pastor*, 97.
68. Baxter, *Reformed Pastor*, 96.
69. Baxter, *Reformed Pastor*, 96.
70. As quoted in Michael S. Lundy and J. I. Packer, eds., *Depression, Anxiety, and the Christian Life: Practical Wisdom from Richard Baxter* (Wheaton, Ill.: Crossway, 2018), 160–61.
71. As quoted in Lundy and Packer, eds., *Depression, Anxiety, and the Christian Life*, 160.

families."[72] He wrote, "If any good be begun by the ministry in any soul, a careless, prayerless, worldly family is like to stifle it, or very much hinder it; whereas, if you could but get the rulers of families to do their duty, to take up the work where you left it, and help it on, what abundance of good might be done!"[73]

Writing

Baxter greatly invested in preaching, counseling, and home visits with families. However, he also devoted much of his time to writing.[74] The writings compiled in his *Practical Works* boast more than four million words, while the rest of his works produce more than six million.[75] Baxter wrote more than 130 books, including enduring classics such as *The Reformed Pastor* (1656), *The Saints' Everlasting Rest* (1650), and *A Call to the Unconverted* (1658), which sold twenty thousand copies in its first year of publication.[76] One author compares Baxter's literary contribution to that of fellow Puritan John Owen. It is noted that Baxter's writings would double the size of Owen's twenty-four volumes.[77] Beeke summarized the theological nature of these publications:

> Baxter's writings are a strange theological mix. He was one of a few Puritans whose doctrines of God's decrees, atonement, and justification were anything but Reformed. Though he generally structured his theology along Reformed lines of thought, he frequently leaned towards Arminian thinking. He developed his own notion of universal redemption, which offended Calvinists, but retained a form of personal election, which offended

---

72. As quoted in Lundy and Packer, eds., *Depression, Anxiety, and the Christian Life*, 100.

73. As quoted in Lundy and Packer, eds., *Depression, Anxiety, and the Christian Life*, 100.

74. Baxter, *Autobiography of Richard Baxter*, 78. Some of the forty-seven books written during his time in Kidderminster include *Aphorisms of Justification and the Covenants*, *The Saints' Everlasting Rest*, and *The Reformed Pastor*.

75. Packer, *Evangelical Influences*, 227.

76. Packer, *Puritan Portraits*, 160.

77. Iain Murray, "Richard Baxter: The Reluctant Puritan?," in *The Westminster Conference 1991: Advancing in Adversity* (London: Westminster Conference, 1991), 1.

Arminians. He rejected reprobation. He was greatly influenced by the Amyraldians and incorporated much of their thinking, including hypothetical universalism, which teaches that Christ hypothetically died for all men, but His death only has real benefit to those who believe. For Baxter, Christ's death was more of a legal satisfaction of the law than a personal substitutionary death on behalf of elect sinners.[78]

Throughout his writings on theology, pastoral ministry, counseling, family, and much more, Baxter's evangelistic heart permeated his publications. Sidney Rooy highlighted this focus, writing, "For Baxter nothing is more urgent than conversion. The stated object of many of his writings, and the repeated application in others, is to press for the believing response of the unconverted."[79]

Baxter used his writing as he did his preaching, catechisms, and counseling. He sought to write in such a way as to strengthen the spiritual state of the families within his church. One author observed, "Baxter's pastoral experience in Kidderminster and writings both before and after the Restoration bear out the theme of ensuring that his parishioners were genuinely Christians."[80]

The Lasting Impact of Baxter's Emphasis on Family Worship

Baxter spent his Kidderminster ministry convinced that family worship is God's will, and he spent these same years encouraging family worship. His prayers were answered as nearly every household under his pastoral leadership embraced and faithfully practiced family worship through prayers, Scripture reading, and teaching catechisms. Kapic and Gleason reported that out of the two thousand adults in Kidderminster, most were saved during Baxter's ministry.[81]

---

78. Beeke and Pederson, *Meet the Puritans*, 66.

79. Rooy, *Theology of Missions*, 71.

80. Paul C. H. Lim, "Puritans and the Church of England: Historiography and Ecclesiology," in *The Cambridge Companion to Puritanism*, ed. John Coffey and Paul C. H. Lim (Cambridge: Cambridge University Press, 2008), 225.

81. Kapic and Gleason, *Devoted Life*, 31.

In 1658, Baxter was able to celebrate what the Lord had done in Kidderminster, writing, "I know not a congregation in England that hath in it proportionately so many that fear God."[82]

The fruit of Baxter's ministry can be measured in many ways. The number of conversions, the number of publications, and the transformation of family worship throughout the town are all markers of this success. Baxter himself described some of the exciting aspects of his Kidderminster tenure: "The congregation was usually full, so that we were fain to build five galleries after my coming. Our private meetings also were full. On the Lord's days there was no disorder to be seen in the streets, but you might hear 100 families singing psalms and repeating sermons as you passed through the streets."[83] Robert Sheehan considered Baxter's ministry in Kidderminster to be the most fruitful of all Puritan pastorates.[84]

Baxter added his own personal observation of the change in the Kidderminster families: "When I came first there was about one family in a street that worshipped God and called on his name, and when I came away there were some streets where there was not passed one family in the side of a street that did not so, and that did not, by professing serious godliness, give us hopes of their sincerity."[85]

This change and growth was not temporary. Baxter was fortunate to enjoy a ministry in which the Lord brought enduring fruit. Beeke wrote, "He could say that of the six hundred converts that were brought to faith under his preaching, he could not name one that had backslidden to the ways of the world."[86]

Marcus Loane noted that George Whitefield wrote on Baxter's lasting impact nearly a century after Baxter completed his ministry in Kidderminster. When Whitefield visited Kidderminster on

---

82. Loane, *Makers of Puritan History*, 184.

83. Baxter, *Autobiography of Richard Baxter*, 79.

84. Robert Sheehan, "The 'Christian Directory' of Richard Baxter," in *The Westminster Conference 1991: Advancing in Adversity* (London: Westminster Conference, 1991), 25.

85. Baxter, *Autobiography of Richard Baxter*, 79.

86. Beeke, *Puritan Evangelism*, 44.

December 31, 1743, he wrote, "I was greatly refreshed to find what a sweet savor of good Mr. Baxter's doctrine, works, and discipline, remained to this day."[87]

---

87. Loane, *Makers of Puritan History*, 183.

CHAPTER SEVEN

Implications for Today's Church and Family Ministry

Although Baxter's writings and ministry took place more than 350 years ago, his theology of family worship carries implications for today's church. As Packer reminded the reader, "If we strip his ideas of their seventeenth-century dress, he has as much to teach us as any man of his day."[1]

Baxter once wrote, "Before I desire anything, I shall know whether it be God's will or not."[2] Baxter sought the will of God and became convinced that family worship was included. He then invested in equipping those around him to practice this discipline. Conviction of the will of God directed his ministry, an example that today's church would do well to follow. Today's church must resolve to zealously desire the will of God and nothing else. Baxter would therefore lead us to pursue family worship.

The impact of family worship reaches beyond the home. Baxter believed the benefits of one spiritually healthy family would touch the surrounding community. This potential fruit was meant to motivate families. Baxter claimed, "Family reformation is the easiest and most likely way to a common reformation."[3] The opposite effect served as a warning. Baxter believed that the effect of an ungodly home would also impact the world surrounding it. He wrote, "It is an evident truth

---

1. Packer, *Redemption and Restoration of Man*, 406.
2. Baxter, *Dying Thoughts*, 75.
3. Baxter, *Godly Home*, 113.

that most of the mischiefs that now infest or seize upon mankind throughout the earth are caused by ill-governed families."[4]

Baxter was not alone in thinking that the neglect of family worship would harm the church. Two years before Baxter's death, the Second London Baptist Confession of 1689 also expressed this warning. The preface claimed that the "one spring and cause of the decay of religion in our day…is the neglect of the worship of God in families."[5]

While many have sought reformation in the home, teaching about family worship alone would always prove insufficient. Baxter sought to lead families to truly practice worship in a way that blessed them and those around them. To this end, he preached, counseled, and wrote on the application of Scripture. As Packer observed, "Baxter wrote far more on the uses of doctrines than on the doctrines themselves."[6] He believed that an application of the theology of family worship would have a lasting impact.

George Hamond also argued for family worship on the basis that it would bring a blessing to the entire congregation, writing, "It is evident that none can more directly and really befriend the church of Christ than they do who are most diligent and faithful in promoting family worship."[7]

Donald Whitney also noted the impact family worship could have on the rest of the church. He concluded, "Since the church is comprised of family units—from singles to large families and everything in between—if the homes are changed through family worship, the church will be changed."[8] Whitney's conviction resonates with Leland Ryken's position: "The health of the church depends on what happens in the family."[9]

---

4. Baxter, *Godly Home*, 112.

5. The 1689 Baptist Confession of Faith, https://www.the1689confession.com/1689/introduction.

6. Packer, *Redemption and Restoration of Man*, 11.

7. Hamond, *Case for Family Worship*, 106–7.

8. Whitney, *Family Worship*, 35.

9. Ryken, *Worldly Saints*, 85.

In light of the consequences of neglect he has seen within the church, Kerry Ptacek has called the modern church to family worship: "After a century without family worship, today's Christian families grow progressively weaker and less resistant to worldly pressures."[10] Ligon Duncan and Terry Johnson also describe this current state, portraying American families as isolated, distracted, worldly, and spiritually dying. These authors suggested that families today may rediscover spiritual vitality by returning to the old paths of family worship. They wrote, "Children growing up with the daily experience of seeing their parents humbled in worship, focusing on spiritual things, submitting to the authority of the Word, catechizing and otherwise instructing their children will not easily turn from Christ."[11]

J. I. Packer also drew a contrast between the Puritan view of family and today's reality. While the Puritans remained spiritually mature, enjoying the Word of God, prayers, and praises in the home, such is no longer common. Packer addressed this disparity and the need for Baxter's conviction today: "In an era in which family life has become brittle even among Christians, with chicken-hearted spouses taking the easy course of separation rather than working at their relationship, and narcissistic parents spoiling their children materially while neglecting them spiritually, there is once more much to be learned from the Puritans' very different ways."[12]

Beeke and Jones observed the current state of family worship and contended that it has become less of a duty that is reflected as God's will and instead is considered a take-it-or-leave-it spiritual discipline. They wrote, "Many Christians today view family devotions…as a matter of Christian liberty. They do not see them as a divinely commanded duty but an opportunity to excel spiritually above what is absolutely required by God."[13]

Beeke further explored the relationship between worship in the home and growth in the church. He attributed the lack of internal

---

10. Ptacek, *Family Worship*, 5.
11. Duncan and Johnson, "Call to Family Worship," 14.
12. Packer, *Quest for Godliness*, 26.
13. Beeke and Jones, *Puritan Theology*, 866.

church growth to a lack of stress on the importance of family worship. "As goes the home, so goes the church, so goes the nation. Family worship is a most decisive factor in how the home goes."[14]

Baxter not only defended family worship as God's will but also modeled how pastors and church leaders can encourage and equip families to practice it faithfully. His example presents a biblical responsibility for church leaders to train families. It remains a matter of discipleship. Great Commission churches will therefore include family worship as one of their discipleship goals and as an important aspect of ministry within the church.

One can only imagine the transformation that could take place if the local church intentionally equipped heads of households to lead in family worship. When these spiritual leaders are trained to lead in teaching the Word of God, praying with their family, and praising the Lord together in the home, one would expect to see a radical revival in both the home and the church. This is exactly the sort of revival that Baxter sought.

In the conclusion of Baxter's encouragement for family worship, he believed he had sufficiently proven that family worship is indeed God's will. "These reasons will seem sufficient to convince them of so sweet, profitable, and necessary a work."[15] He believed he had labored to a great extent to this end, if not perhaps more extensively than needed: "I have been more tedious on this subject than a holy, hungry Christian possibly may think necessary who needs not so many arguments to persuade him to feast his soul with God and to delight himself in the frequent exercises of faith and love."[16] Although Baxter believed that family worship is man's duty, he did not consider it to be an unhappy burden. Instead, it is something to be enjoyed. Baxter wrote, "A holy, well-governed family tends not only to the safety of the members but also to the ease and pleasure of their lives...what a sweet and happy life is this! It is the closest thing to heaven on earth."[17]

---

14. Beeke, *Family Worship*, 2.
15. Baxter, *Godly Home*, 97.
16. Baxter, *Godly Home*, 97.
17. Baxter, *Godly Home*, 107.

Further Encouragement for Family Worship

While Baxter's biblical defense for family worship has driven the previous chapters, it has been presented with the hope of encouraging modern families to cultivate this practice. The Scriptures offered throughout Baxter's argument are meant to spur us on to obey the Word of God and enjoy the blessings of worship in the home. Therefore, allow me to offer some final, practical words of encouragement for family worship.

Five Blessings Prayerful Families Enjoy

Family worship exists when we see a faithful teaching of the Word of God, shared praises, and joint prayers in the home. Many Christians begin introducing family worship by implementing a consistent rhythm of prayer. Countless blessings come when prayer is valued and shared in the home. My hope is that these five blessings will encourage you in this joyful discipline.

Prayer Brings Worship into the Home

When Jesus taught His disciples how to pray, He taught them to begin with a heart of worship, recognizing the holiness of the Father, praying, "Our Father which art in heaven, hallowed be thy name" (Matt. 6:9). Prayer affords us the opportunity to adore the Lord together. We exalt His name and honor Him. We praise Him for who He is and all He has done. Our hearts are filled with gratitude and worship as our homes are filled with prayer.

Prayer Finds Families Seeking the Lord's Guidance Together
The Lord's Prayer continues with the famous line "Thy kingdom come, thy will be done in earth, as it is in heaven" (Matt. 6:10). Jesus taught His disciples to seek the will of the Father through their prayers. In the same way, families that pray together seek the Lord's will for their homes and hearts together. When a household makes time to pray with one another, they find unique opportunities to seek the Lord's guidance for their lives.

Prayer Finds Families Seeking the Lord's Provision Together
The next verse of the model prayer reads, "Give us this day our daily bread." Jesus taught His disciples to pray for the Lord's provision daily. Families today are to follow this example. Every home has daily needs for provision. This includes our need for groceries, jobs, housing, patience, wisdom, peace, and much more. Jesus says that "your heavenly Father knoweth that ye have need of all these things" (Matt. 6:32). Since families share these needs, they ought to share this prayer. In prayer, the needs of our hearts are trusted in the hands of our Father.

Prayer Finds Families Seeking Forgiveness Together
Jesus continues His teaching on prayer, saying, "and forgive us our debts, as we forgive our debtors" (Matt. 6:12). Most days find most family members needing to forgive and needing to be forgiven. These needs appropriately lead us to prayer.

Instead of offering the quick apology or even leaving it unspoken, families who cultivate regular rhythms of prayer will find beautiful opportunities to genuinely seek forgiveness together. Such intimacy and honesty in our prayer lives will surely bring blessings to the home.

Prayer Finds Families Seeking Deliverance Together
We are taught to go to the Father in prayer, asking for deliverance as we pray, "Lead us not into temptation, but deliver us from evil" (Matt. 6:13). Every home faces temptation. Every home faces the

attacks of the enemy and the pull of the flesh. Therefore, every family can find tremendous blessing in coming before the Father together regularly in prayer. For when deliverance, protection, freedom, and victory are needs, prayers are vital.

An Encouragement to Begin Leading Your Family in Prayer
I am convinced that prayer is one of the most powerful and greatest blessings we could ever bring through the front doors of our homes. It is a habit worth cultivating, a spiritual discipline worth practicing, and an aspect of family worship worth enjoying.

One way to begin implementing prayer in the home is to lead your family in one prayer a day. Whether you pray with your spouse before work, with your children as they get ready for bed, or the entire family over dinner during family worship, daily prayers can breathe life into the rhythm of the home in a way that nothing else can.

Perhaps you can even begin with the prayer discussed in this chapter. Simply gather your family and pray, "Our Father which art in heaven, hallowed be thy name. Thy kingdom come, thy will be done in earth, as it is in heaven. Give us this day our daily bread. And forgive us our debts, as we forgive our debtors. And lead us not into temptation, but deliver us from evil" (Matt. 6:9–13).

Five Blessings Thankful Families Enjoy

Just as prayer is at the heart of family worship, thanksgiving is at the heart of prayer. Families who give thanks together will enjoy the blessings of a gratitude-filled home. What a joy this can be, especially in a culture where so much is taken for granted! When families learn to cultivate thankful hearts from day to day, these five attributes will also find their way into the home.

Gratitude Cultivates Contentment
One of the surest ways to combat consumerism, overcome the temptation of materialism, abstain from coveting what your friends have, and avoid complaining is to become a thankful family. Thankful

families spend more time giving thanks for the blessings they do have instead of chasing the things they do not.

Thankful families cultivate gratitude in their hearts and homes, which leads to the sort of contentment Paul wrote about in Philippians: "I have learned, in whatsoever state I am, therewith to be content. I know both how to be abased, and I know how to abound: every where and in all things I am instructed both to be full and to be hungry, both to abound and to suffer need. I can do all things through Christ which strengtheneth me" (Phil. 4:11–13).

Gratitude Cultivates Humility
Gratitude is a constant reminder that all we need comes from someone else. We are ultimately not the ones providing for our families—God is. We give thanks to the Lord, recognizing our dependence on Him. What a humbling recognition! Pride flees from the heart of gratitude, and humility settles in right next to thanksgiving.

Gratitude Cultivates Joy
Families that spend time counting their blessings will quickly see that joy follows gratitude. Even on the days when joy seems elusive, a time of thanksgiving can beautifully remind us that we are still blessed. We still have reason to give thanks and rejoice, and these reasons can fill us with joy. We see this relationship between gratitude and joy when Paul calls us to "rejoice in the Lord always" (Phil. 4:4) and then immediately follows this command with a plea to fill our prayers with thanksgiving. When our prayers are thankful, our hearts are joyful.

Gratitude Cultivates Perseverance
Several Scriptures call the followers of Christ to maintain a heart of gratitude, no matter what. Paul expresses this at least twice, writing, "In every thing give thanks" (1 Thess. 5:18) and "In every thing by prayer and supplication with thanksgiving let your requests be made known unto God" (Phil. 4:6).

What a challenge! For many families this might even seem impossible. How can we be thankful in all circumstances when some of those circumstances are tragic? How can our prayers be filled with thanksgiving for everything when that "everything" includes heart-breaking loss? How can we celebrate Thanksgiving when we have lost loved ones, battled sicknesses, suffered unemployment, struggled in our marriages, and fought with our children? What is there to be thankful for in these circumstances?

Yet there again, we find the biblical call to give thanks. We find biblical examples of families who gave thanks in the midst of suffering, loss, mourning, grief, and persecution, and by maintaining this spirit of gratitude, they cultivated perseverance through the storm. As they grieved and mourned, they also worshiped, and the Lord carried them through.

In the Old Testament, a man named Job lost everything. His seven sons and three daughters all died, and he lost all he owned. Even still, from this pit of despair, he persevered because he maintained a level of gratitude and praise, worshiping God: "Then Job arose, and rent his mantle, and shaved his head, and fell down upon the ground, and worshipped, and said, Naked came I out of my mother's womb, and naked shall I return thither: the LORD gave, and the LORD hath taken away; blessed be the name of the LORD" (Job 1:20–21).

Another example of gratitude encouraging perseverance is found in the New Testament when Paul and Silas were bound in prison. They were beaten with rods, inflicted with many blows, and thrown into prison with their feet fastened in the stocks. Yet they persevered, for they never stopped worshiping. They had cultivated gratitude that continued to overflow even out of their jail cell: "At midnight Paul and Silas prayed, and sang praises unto God: and the prisoners heard them" (Acts 16:25).

All families face storms and walk through seasons of pain, grief, hardship, and suffering. Even in the midst of such days, a blessing remains for the family that comes together in family worship and lifts up prayers of thanksgiving, praising God for His presence in the storm and His promise to never leave us nor forsake us.

Gratitude Cultivates Worship

We have all heard it said that "families who pray together, stay together." Let us also say, "families who give thanks together, worship together." Giving thanks to God is worship, and therefore a family who sets out to cultivate a home of gratitude will immediately find they have also encouraged a home of worship.

These are the families that see the grace of God reaching the hearts of their home, which causes thanksgiving to "redound to the glory of God" (2 Cor. 4:15). Our thanksgiving glorifies God. O that families today would come together in family worship and enjoy gratitude-filled homes and discover the blessings of contentment, humility, joy, perseverance, and worship!

Three Testimonies to Share with Your Children

As you cultivate a rhythm of family prayers and seek hearts of gratitude, I encourage you to also begin reading and teaching the Bible together. This discipline allows families to hear, understand, obey, and enjoy the gospel of Jesus Christ while growing in their relationship with the Lord. As you teach these gospel truths, I want to offer a practical way to share your own testimony with your children. Such testimonies allow them to see a practical example of gospel transformation.

Most parents would probably say they know their children very well. We have watched them grow up and have shared in just about every significant milestone they have enjoyed so far. We have watched their physical, mental, emotional, and spiritual growth. We know what makes them laugh and what makes them cry. We have seen them make new friends, travel to new places, and even try new foods. We know their favorite toy, their favorite book, and their favorite movie. But how well do your kids know you?

As we continue to get to know the hearts and stories of our children, let us not miss the opportunity to share our hearts and stories with them. As you gather for family worship, consider sharing these three testimonies with your children.

Tell Your Children the Story of How Jesus Saved You
Have you ever shared your testimony with your children? When we tell our kids how the Lord saved us from our sin and gave us new life, we invite them to celebrate salvation with us and provide a personal example of the power of the gospel.

Paul was not ashamed of the gospel, for he believed it is "the power of God unto salvation to every one that believeth" (Rom. 1:16). He knew this salvation and frequently shared his testimony. Paul would often recount his old life, his encounter with Jesus Christ, and the radical transformation He brought to his life (Acts 22:3–16; 26:4–23; Gal. 1:13–23).

Perhaps you could read some of Paul's testimonies with your children during family worship and then share your own testimony with your family, letting them hear the story of how Jesus rescued you from your former way of life and made you a new creation.

Tell Your Children How God Has Worked Mightily in Your Life
After God led Joshua and His people across the Jordan, God had the people set up twelve memorial stones. These stones were meant to serve as a reminder of God's mighty works. The Lord ensured that Israel would pass down this testimony to the coming generations.

Joshua said to the people, "When your children ask their fathers in time to come, saying, What mean ye by these stones? Then ye shall answer them, That the waters of Jordan were cut off before the ark of the covenant of the LORD…these stones shall be for a memorial unto the children of Israel for ever" (Josh. 4:6–7).

What a blessing it would be if you were able to set up some "memorial stones" in your home by finding opportunities to share testimonies with your children! Tell them about the mighty ways in which God has worked in your life. Tell them stories of how the Lord answered prayers. You have probably never followed the Lord through the Jordan, but you can share testimonies of the many times the Lord has led and guided you. Think of one of these testimonies and then write a word or two on a stone and set the rock on the kitchen table. I imagine that in less than a few hours, one of your children will see the rock and ask you, "What does this mean to you?"

Tell Your Children How God Carried You through Difficult Times
As we seek to disciple our children and as we pray for their spiritual maturity, we want to prepare their hearts for the difficult seasons that will inevitably come. We know they will face hardship and heartache. We know they will suffer and grieve. And we know that the Lord can carry them through it all.

One way we can teach our children to find refuge and shelter in the Lord, trusting Him in the darkest of days, is to share our own testimonies of times when the Lord carried us through such storms. How did you seek the Lord during a season of loss? How did God provide when you were unemployed? How do you cry out to Him when your heart is heavy with grief or anxiety? How do you find strength in the Lord in the face of persecution? How do you come to know the Lord as the God of comfort? How has Jesus proven faithful even when no one else was there?

I love how Paul shares one of these testimonies with the church, writing, "We are troubled on every side, yet not distressed; we are perplexed, but not in despair; persecuted, but not forsaken; cast down, but not destroyed; always bearing about in the body the dying of the Lord Jesus, that the life also of Jesus might be made manifest in our body" (2 Cor. 4:8–10).

The Lord has moved in our lives. He has saved, forgiven, provided, healed, restored, delivered, and blessed. He has answered prayers beyond anything we could have imagined. Now let us be faithful to share these stories with our children as we declare, "We will not hide them from their children, shewing to the generation to come the praises of the LORD, and his strength, and his wonderful works that he hath done…that they might set their hope in God, and not forget the works of God, but keep his commandments" (Ps. 78:4, 7).

How Family Worship Blesses Us with Family Time

Testimonies, prayers, shared praises, and a faithful teaching of the Word of God remain some of the hallmarks of family worship. These bring countless blessings to the home. There are other blessings, however, that families will also enjoy, for family worship is a call we see woven throughout Scripture, filled with blessings for the entire home. One of these blessings seems especially applicable for those who feel burdened by busy weeks and full calendars. In a culture that seems to leave families in a constant battle for their schedules, we rejoice over one blessing that family worship brings—time together.

A family that prays together, sings praises together, and enjoys reading the Bible together will inevitably find themselves blessed with more time together. When we read the famous words of Deuteronomy 6:4–9, we not only catch a glimpse of family worship but also see that family time is assumed in any home that consistently enjoys worshiping together.

This passage describes a family that engages in discipleship while sitting in the house together, walking together, and spending time together upon waking up in the mornings and before going to sleep in the evenings.

We need to bring family worship through the front doors of our homes. We need to welcome this natural rhythm and overcome the challenges we face while living in a culture that finds family meals uncommon and family conversations just as rare.

Family worship cultivates a pattern that invites everyone in the home to push aside all distractions, take a break from all media, and just be still in the presence of God and one another for a few minutes every day. It simultaneously strengthens our relationship with the Lord and our relationships with our spouse and children.

It is not enough to just carve out time together, for some of the most stressed-out families are sprinting through life together, all the while missing out on any profound connection or significant conversation. Just because we are in the same room, at the same restaurant, stuck in the same traffic, or running the same errands does not guarantee that we are on the same page or growing together as a family.

Family worship does not just produce family time. It produces *meaningful* family time. When a family engages the Word of God together, shares prayer requests together, or enjoys worship music together, there is a deeper connection as hearts are opened and real life, real concerns, real fears, real hopes, and real needs all begin to trump the ever-busy calendar.

A Sample Guide for Family Worship

Central Passage: Matthew 7:24–27

Catechism:

- Question: What do the Scriptures principally teach?

- Answer: The Scriptures principally teach what man is to believe concerning God, and what duty God requires of man.[1]

- Application: The Bible is more than just a book. It is the Word of God; therefore, it is not just something we read, but it is meant to lead us to belief and obedience. Today's devotion will remind us of this call to obey the Word of God as a family.

Family Praise Playlist

As you enjoy the Word of God together this week, focus on one of these worship songs and consider creating a new playlist that may serve as your family soundtrack this week:

- "How Firm a Foundation," by John Rippon
- "Speak, O Lord," by Keith and Kristyn Getty
- "Word of God Speak," by Bart Millard and Pete Kipley

You can find these songs on your favorite music app and listen together as a family, look up the lyrics so you can sing together, or play

---

1. Charles H. Spurgeon, *Spurgeon's Catechism: With Scriptural Proofs* (Apollo, Pa.: Ichthus Publications, 2014), 11. Both the question and the answer are quoted from the third question in Spurgeon's catechism.

these worship songs in the home throughout the week while you are cooking, playing outside, getting ready for the day, riding in the car, working in the garage, doing homework, or any other weekly activity.

Family Time in the Word of God

As you gather the family for worship, open the Bible to Matthew 7 and read the central passage together:

> Therefore whosoever heareth these sayings of mine, and doeth them, I will liken him unto a wise man, which built his house upon a rock: and the rain descended, and the floods came, and the winds blew, and beat upon that house; and it fell not: for it was founded upon a rock. And every one that heareth these sayings of mine, and doeth them not, shall be likened unto a foolish man, which built his house upon the sand: and the rain descended, and the floods came, and the winds blew, and beat upon that house; and it fell: and great was the fall of it. (Matt. 7:24–27)

Family Teaching

This passage comes at the end of the Sermon on the Mount. Jesus preached on a variety of topics, including anger, lust, love, giving, praying, and fasting. In the coming days, you might consider walking through this entire sermon with your family during worship (Matt. 5–7). Jesus concludes His sermon with a call to obedience. The crowds have heard His sermon, but they are wise if they obey all they have heard. This truth is also reflected in James 1:22 when James calls Christians to "be ye doers of the word, and not hearers only."

In Matthew 7, Jesus paints a clear picture of the difference between a life founded on obedience to God's Word and one that is founded on disobedience to it. It is the difference between one who is wise and one who is foolish, between one who stands firm and one who falls and is destroyed.

Two foundational truths at the end of Jesus's Sermon on the Mount may be applied to families today. In Matthew 7:24–27, Jesus draws a contrast between those who obey and those who disobey the

Word of God. Since Jesus uses the illustration of houses, a natural application can be applied to homes today—namely, that all families will encounter storms in this life, and only families founded on obedience to the Word of God will stand. These are the wise builders who dig deep and construct a strong foundation.[2]

Storms of culture, temptation, and sin will beat against our homes. The same storm comes on both houses here. Storms of life will be different each time, and these storms are unpredictable. If our foundation is fickle, then the storms will destroy our lives. Our foundation must be something that is consistent, firm, steadfast, unchanging, and true. God's Word must be our foundation. To set His Word as the foundation of our lives is to hear it and obey.

Family Discussion

After teaching the Scriptures to your family, invite them to respond. Ask a few discussion questions about the passage. The nature of these questions will often depend on the ages of those present. Here are some sample questions to follow the Matthew 7 passage:

1. What are some things we have read in the Bible that we need to obey?
2. What makes obedience to God difficult sometimes?
3. Can you remember a time when you disobeyed the Lord?
4. What should we do when we disobey God?
5. What blessings do you think we would enjoy if we obeyed God?
6. How can our family set the Word of God as the foundation of our home?

Family Prayer

Close this time of family worship with prayer. You can either pray over your family or take a moment to allow each member of the household to share any prayer requests or praises that might be on

---

2. John R. W. Stott, *The Message of the Sermon on the Mount* (Downers Grove, Ill.: InterVarsity Press, 1978), 208.

their hearts. You can also invite others to pray or even go around and have each person say a prayer. Over time, family members will likely become more comfortable praying out loud as worship becomes a consistent rhythm in the home. Here is a sample prayer:

> Lord, we praise You for all of our family blessings. Thank You for Your promise to never leave us or forsake us. We believe that You are here with us right now. There is no one like You. There is no Savior but You, Jesus Christ. And we pray that our family will be founded on Your Word. Lead us to obey Your Word for our joy and Your glory. Forgive us for the times when we have disobeyed You and sinned against You. We ask that You will protect us during the storms of life and draw us daily closer to You.

Opportunities for Reflection: Discussion Questions

Reflection on the Abundant Opportunities for Family Worship

1. What Bible verses encourage family worship?

2. What opportunities does your family have to worship together each week?

3. When could you bring your family together for a time of worship in the home?

4. What challenges would you expect to face as you try to implement family worship?

5. What blessings would you expect to see in your home as you practice worshiping together?

Reflection on the Opportunities for Teaching the Word of God

1. What Scriptures do we expect our children to obey? Have we taught these Scriptures well in the home?

2. What are some of the most important Bible stories that you want to teach to your family?

3. How can we create more opportunities to teach our families about the birth, life, death, and resurrection of Jesus?

4. Do our family members have the opportunity to ask questions about what they find in Scripture?

5. When the call to teach the Bible seems overwhelming, how can we depend on the Lord for this ministry?

6. How can we grow in our ability to teach the Word of God?

Reflection on Filling the Home with Prayer and Praises

1. What are the primary elements of family worship? Which of these would be the easiest for you to begin practicing with your family? Which of these would be the most challenging?

2. What Bible verses encourage family prayer?

3. What is the relationship between teaching the Word of God and prayer?

4. Do you currently have a consistent rhythm of family prayer with those in your household? Do you pray with your spouse? Do you pray with your children?

5. Who is currently leading your family in prayer and praises?

6. Do your children have space to share their prayer requests and praises? What would prevent you from praying with them as they share? Who can you ask to hold you accountable to make the most of these opportunities?

7. When is your family able to participate in singing worship songs?

8. How would you describe your prayers before each meal? How would you like to see these mature?

9. What needs do you currently have that should be lifted up in joint family prayer?

10. What would help your family grow in your time of prayer?

Bibliography

BOOKS

Adams, Jay E. *Christian Living in the Home*. Phillipsburg, N.J.: P&R Publishing, 1972.

Akin, Daniel L., ed. *A Theology for the Church*. Nashville, Tenn.: B&H Academic, 2007.

Alexander, James W. *Thoughts on Family Worship*. Tomball, Tex.: Legacy Ministry Publications, 2010.

Anthony, Michael, and Michelle Anthony, eds. *A Theology for Family Ministries*. Nashville, Tenn.: B&H Academic, 2011.

Baxter, Richard. *The Autobiography of Richard Baxter*. New York: E. P. Dutton & Co., 1931.

————. *A Christian Directory or, A Sum of Practical Theology, and Cases of Conscience, Part 2: Christian Economics*. Independently published, 2018.

————. *Dying Thoughts*. Carlisle, Pa.: Banner of Truth, 2004.

————. *The Godly Home*. Wheaton, Ill.: Crossway, 2010.

————. *The Practical Works of Richard Baxter: Selected Treatises*. Peabody, Mass.: Hendrickson, 2010.

————. *A Puritan Catechism for Families*. Bellingham, Wash.: Lexham Press, 2017.

————. *The Reformed Pastor*. Carlisle, Pa.: Banner of Truth, 2005.

Beeke, Joel R. *Family Worship*. Grand Rapids: Reformation Heritage, 2009.

————. *How Should Men Lead Their Families?* Grand Rapids: Reformation Heritage, 2014.

————. *Puritan Evangelism: A Biblical Approach.* 2nd edition. Grand Rapids: Reformation Heritage, 2017.

————. *Reformed Preaching: Proclaiming God's Word from the Heart of the Preacher to the Heart of His People.* Wheaton, Ill.: Crossway, 2018.

Beeke, Joel R., and Mark Jones. *A Puritan Theology: Doctrine for Life.* Grand Rapids: Reformation Heritage, 2012.

Beeke, Joel R., and Randall J. Pederson. *Meet the Puritans: With a Guide to Modern Reprints.* Grand Rapids: Reformation Heritage, 2006.

Bennett, Arthur, ed. *The Valley of Vision: A Collection of Puritan Prayers and Devotions.* Carlisle, Pa.: Banner of Truth, 2017.

Block, Daniel I. *For the Glory of God: Recovering a Biblical Theology of Worship.* Grand Rapids: Baker Academic, 2014.

Brown, John. *Puritan Preaching in England: A Study of Past and Present.* New York: Charles Scribner's Sons, 1900.

Brown, Scott, and Jeff Pollard, eds. *A Theology of the Family: Five Centuries of Biblical Wisdom for Family Life.* Wake Forest, N.C.: NCFIC, 2016.

Bunyan, John. *Bunyan's Catechism.* Choteau, Mont.: Old Paths Gospel Press, 2008.

Coffey, John, and Paul C. H. Lim, eds. *The Cambridge Companion to Puritanism.* Cambridge: Cambridge University Press, 2008.

Davies, Horton. *The Worship of the English Puritans.* Morgan, Pa.: Soli Deo Gloria Publications, 1997.

Deckard, Mark. *Helpful Truth in Past Places: The Puritan Practice of Biblical Counseling.* Fearn, Ross-shire, U.K.: Mentor, 2016.

Enns, Paul P. *The Moody Handbook of Theology.* Chicago: Moody Press, 1989.

Frame, John M. *Systematic Theology: An Introduction to Christian Belief.* Phillipsburg, N.J.: P&R Publishing, 2013.

Grudem, Wayne. *Systematic Theology: An Introduction to Biblical Doctrine.* Grand Rapids: Zondervan, 1994.

————. *Tyndale New Testament Commentaries: 1 Peter.* Downers Grove, Ill.: InterVarsity Press, 2009.

Hamond, George. *The Case for Family Worship*. Orlando, Fla.: Soli Deo Gloria Publications, 2005.

Henry, Matthew. *A Church in the House: Restoring Daily Worship to the Christian Household*. San Antonio, Tex.: Vision Forum, 2007.

Heywood, Oliver. *A Family Altar Erected to the Honour of the Eternal God, or, A Solemn Essay to Promote the Worship of God in Private Houses Being Some Meditations on Genesis 35:2–3*. England: EEBO Editions ProQuest, 2011.

Horn, Cornelia B., and John W. Martens. *Let the Little Children Come to Me: Childhood and Children in Early Christianity*. Washington, D.C.: Catholic University of America Press, 2009.

Jones, Timothy Paul, ed. *Perspectives on Family Ministry: 3 Views*. Nashville, Tenn.: B&H Academic, 2009.

Kapic, Kelly M., and Randall C. Gleason. *The Devoted Life: An Invitation to the Puritan Classics*. Downers Grove, Ill.: InterVarsity Press, 2004.

Keach, Benjamin. *Keach's Catechism*. Edinburgh: CrossReach Publications, 2017.

Köstenberger, Andreas J., with David W. Jones. *God, Marriage, and Family: Rebuilding the Biblical Foundation*. 2nd ed. Wheaton, Ill.: Crossway, 2004.

Lewis, C. S. *Mere Christianity*. New York: Touchstone, 1996.

Lloyd-Jones, D. M. *The Puritans: Their Origins and Successors*. Carlisle, Pa.: Banner of Truth, 2016.

Loane, Marcus L. *Makers of Puritan History*. Grand Rapids: Baker, 1980.

Lumpkin, William L. *Baptist Confessions of Faith*. Valley Forge, Pa.: Judson Press, 1969.

Lundy, Michael S., and J. I. Packer. *Depression, Anxiety, and the Christian Life: Practical Wisdom from Richard Baxter*. Wheaton, Ill.: Crossway, 2018.

Masters, Peter. *The Baptist Confession of Faith 1689: The Second London Confession with Scripture Proofs from the Edition of C. H. Spurgeon, 1855*. London: Wakeman Trust, 2008.

Joseph Mede. *Churches, That Is, Appropriate Places for Christian Worship Both in, and Ever since the Apostles Times. A Discourse at First More Briefly Delivered at a College Chapel, and Since Enlarged.* Oxford Text Archive, p. 25. http://ota.ox.ac.uk/id/A07381.

Moo, Douglas J. *The New International Commentary on the New Testament: The Epistle to the Romans.* Grand Rapids: Eerdmans, 1996.

———. *The Pillar New Testament Commentary: The Letters to the Colossians and to Philemon.* Grand Rapids: Eerdmans, 2008.

Nuttall, Geoffrey F. *Richard Baxter.* London: Thomas Nelson, 1965.

Packer, J. I. *Evangelical Influences: Profiles of Figures and Movements Rooted in the Reformation.* Peabody, Mass.: Hendrickson, 1999.

———. *Puritan Portraits.* Fearn, Ross-shire, U.K.: Christian Focus Publications, 2012.

———. *A Quest for Godliness: The Puritan Vision of the Christian Life.* Wheaton, Ill.: Crossway, 1990.

———. *The Redemption and Restoration of Man in the Thought of Richard Baxter.* Carlisle, U.K.: Paternoster Press, 2003.

Packer, J. I., and Gary A. Parrett. *Grounded in the Gospel: Building Believers the Old-Fashioned Way.* Grand Rapids: Baker, 2010.

Piper, John, and Wayne Grudem, eds. *Recovering Biblical Manhood and Womanhood: A Response to Evangelical Feminism.* Wheaton, Ill.: Crossway, 2012.

Ptacek, Kerry. *Family Worship: Biblical Basis, Historical Reality, and Current Need.* Taylors, S.C.: Southern Presbyterian Press, 2000.

Rogers, Jack. *Presbyterian Creeds: A Guide to the Book of Confessions.* Louisville, Ky.: Westminster John Knox Press, 1991.

Rooy, Sidney H. *The Theology of Missions in the Puritan Tradition: A Study of Representative Puritans: Richard Sibbes, Richard Baxter, John Eliot, Cotton Mather & Jonathan Edwards.* Grand Rapids: Eerdmans, 2006.

Ryken, Leland. *Worldly Saints: The Puritans as They Really Were.* Grand Rapids: Zondervan, 1990.

Schücking, Levin L. *The Puritan Family: A Social Study from the Literary Sources.* New York: Schocken Books, 1970.

The 1689 Baptist Confession of Faith. https://www.the1689confession .com/1689/introduction.

Sproul, R. C. *What Is the Church?* Orlando: Reformation Trust, 2013.

Spurgeon, Charles H.. *Come Ye Children: Obtaining Our Lord's Heart for Loving and Teaching Children.* Abbotsford, Wis.: Aneko Press, 2017.

———. *A Puritan Catechism with Proofs.* Lexington, Ky.: Legacy Publications, 2011.

———. *Spurgeon's Catechism: With Scriptural Proofs.* Apollo, Pa.: Ichthus Publications, 2014.

Stinson, Randy, and Timothy Paul Jones, eds. *Trained in the Fear of God.* Grand Rapids: Kregel, 2011.

Stott, John. *The Message of the Sermon on the Mount.* Downers Grove, Ill.: InterVarsity Press, 1978.

Um, Stephen T. *Preaching the Word: 1 Corinthians, the Word of the Cross.* Wheaton, Ill.: Crossway, 2015.

Whitney, Donald. *Family Worship.* Wheaton, Ill.: Crossway, 2016.

Williamson, G. I. *The Westminster Shorter Catechism.* Phillipsburg, N.J.: P&R Publishing, 2003.

ARTICLES, CHAPTERS, AND SERMONS

Adams, Richard. "What Are the Duties of Parents and Children; and How Are They to Be Managed According to Scripture?" In *Puritan Sermons, 1659–1689.* Vol. 2. Wheaton, Ill.: Richard Owen Roberts, 1981.

Alexander, "The Father and Family Worship." In Pollard and Brown, *Theology of the Family.*

Anthony, Michelle D. "Equipping Parents to Be the Spiritual Leaders in the Home." In *A Theology for Family Ministries.* Edited by Michael Anthony and Michelle Anthony. Nashville, Tenn.: B&H Academic, 2011.

Baxter, Richard. "The Cure of Melancholy and Overmuch Sorrow." In *Puritan Sermons, 1659–1689*. Vol. 3. Wheaton, Ill.: Richard Owen Roberts, 1981.

———. "What Light Must Shine in Our Works?" In *Puritan Sermons, 1659–1689*. Vol. 2. Wheaton, Ill.: Richard Owen Roberts, 1981.

Beougher, Timothy K. "Richard Baxter (1615–1691): A Model of Pastoral Leadership for Evangelism and Church Growth." *The Southern Baptist Journal of Theology* 6, no. 4 (Winter 2002).

Blanchette, Leon M., Jr. "Spiritual Markers in the Life of a Child." In *A Theology for Family Ministries*. Nashville, Tenn.: B&H Academic, 2011.

Cook, Paul. "The Life and Work of a Minister According to the Puritans." In *Puritan Papers, Volume One: 1956–1959*. Edited by J. I. Packer. Phillipsburg, N.J.: P&R Publishing, 2000.

Dever, Mark E. "The Church." In *A Theology for the Church*. Edited by Daniel L. Akin. Nashville, Tenn.: B&H Academic, 2007.

Doolittle, Thomas. "How May the Duty of Daily Family Prayer Be Best Managed for the Spiritual Benefit of Everyone in the Family?" In *Puritan Sermons, 1659–1689*. Vol. 2. Wheaton, Ill.: Richard Owen Roberts, 1981.

———. "Seven Reasons Families Should Pray." In Pollard and Brown, *Theology of the Family*.

———. "The Word of God and Family Prayer." In Pollard and Brown, *Theology of the Family*.

Duncan, Ligon, and Terry Johnson. "A Call to Family Worship." *Journal for Biblical Manhood and Womanhood* 9, no. 1 (Spring 2004).

Jones, Timothy Paul. "How a Biblical Worldview Shapes the Way We Teach Our Children." *The Journal of Discipleship and Family Ministry: Equipping the Generations for Gospel-Centered Living* 4, no. 1 (Fall/Winter 2013).

Lim, Paul C. H. "Puritans and the Church of England: Historiography and Ecclesiology." In *The Cambridge Companion to Puritanism*. Edited by John Coffey and Paul C. H. Lim. Cambridge: Cambridge University Press, 2008.

Lye, Thomas. "By What Scriptural Rules May Catechizing Be So Managed, as That It May Become Most Universally Profitable?" In *Puritan Sermons: 1659–1689*. Vol. 2. Wheaton, Ill.: Richard Owen Roberts, 1981.

———. "What May Gracious Parents Best Do for the Conversion of Those Children Whose Wickedness Is Occasioned by Their Sinful Severity or Indulgence?" In *Puritan Sermons, 1659–1689*. Vol. 3. Wheaton, Ill.: Richard Owen Roberts, 1981.

Murray, Iain. "Richard Baxter: The Reluctant Puritan?" In *The Westminster Conference 1991: Advancing in Adversity*. London: Westminster Conference, 1991.

Murray, John J. "The Puritan Brotherhood." In *The Westminster Conference 1991: Advancing in Adversity*. London: Westminster Conference, 1991.

Packer, J. I. "The Puritan Approach to Worship." In *Puritan Papers, Volume Three: 1963–1964*. Edited by J. I. Packer. Phillipsburg, N.J.: P&R Publishing, 2001.

Plumer, William S. "The Lord's Day at Home." In Pollard and Brown, *Theology of the Family: Five Centuries of Biblical Wisdom for Family Life*. Edited by Jeff Pollard and Scott T. Brown. Wake Forest, N.C.: NCFIC, 2016.

Poythress, Vern S. "The Church as Family: Why Male Leadership in the Family Requires Male Leadership in the Church." In Piper and Grudem, *Recovering Biblical Manhood and Womanhood*.

Robinson, C. Jeffrey, Sr. "The Home Is an Earthly Kingdom." In *Trained in the Fear of God: Family Ministry in Theological, Historical, and Practical Perspective*. Edited by Randy Stinson and Timothy Paul Jones. Grand Rapids: Kregel, 2011.

Samuel, Leith. "Richard Baxter and 'The Saints' Everlasting Rest." In *The Westminster Conference 1991: Advancing in Adversity*. London: Westminster Conference, 1991.

Sheehan, Robert. "The 'Christian Directory' of Richard Baxter" In *The Westminster Conference 1991: Advancing in Adversity*. London: Westminster Conference, 1991.

Steele, Richard. "What Are the Duties of Husbands and Wives towards Each Other?" In *Puritan Sermons, 1659–1689*. Vol. 2. Wheaton, Ill.: Richard Owen Roberts, 1981.

Strother, Jay. "Family-Equipping Ministry: Church and Home as Cochampions." In *Perspectives on Family Ministry: 3 Views*. Edited by Timothy Paul Jones. Nashville, Tenn.: B&H Academic, 2009.

Wilson, J. Lewis. "Catechisms and the Puritans." In *Puritan Papers, Volume Four: 1965–1967*. Edited by J. I. Packer. Phillipsburg, N.J.: P&R Publishing, 2004.

Young, W. "The Puritan Principle of Worship." In *Puritan Papers, Volume One: 1956–1959*. Edited by J. I. Packer. Phillipsburg, N.J.: P&R Publishing, 2000.

DISSERTATIONS

Anderson, Jody Kent. "The Church within the Church: An Examination of Family Worship in Puritan Thought." Mid-America Baptist Theological Seminary, 2009.

Brown, Sylvia Monica. "Godly Household Government from Perkins to Milton: The Rhetoric and Politics of Oeconomia, 1600–1645." Princeton University, 1994.

Doriani, Daniel. "The Godly Household in Puritan Theology 1560–1640." Westminster Theological Seminary, 1986.

Mair, Nathaniel Harrington. "Christian Sanctification and Individual Pastoral Care in Richard Baxter." Union Theological Seminary, 1967.

McCan, Robert L. "The Conception of the Church in Richard Baxter and John Bunyan: A Comparison and Contrast." University of Edinburgh, 1955. https://www.era.lib.ed.ac.uk /handle/1842/35192.

Miller, Donald G. "A Critical Appraisal of Richard Baxter's Views of the Church and Their Applicability to Contemporary Church Problems." New York University, 1935.

Subject Index